MJS & Mac 333

BOOK OF TRINITY

Third Eclipse

MJS   Mac 333 & Master InOut
SUDOKU SET
Book 3

for Children
even if they are Adults

\

TABLE OF CONTENTS

VOLUME 1

CRYSTAL REALM

PART / MOVEMENT / JUMP 1 : *La Journée Crystale*

PART / MOVEMENT / JUMP 2 : *Eclipse of the Earth*

Triple Trebled Show

VOLUME 2

Triple Trebled Show

PART / MOVEMENT / JUMP **3** : *ALCHEMY*

EPILOGUE

\

Dramatis Personae

ZENSEN

CRYSTAL CHIP

DREAM CHILD

DREAM WOMAN

DREAM MAN

BORDERLINE

CRYSTAL MAN

CRYSTAL WOMAN

CRYSTAL CHILD

CRYSTAL BIOCHIP

CRYSTAL SHE

CRYSTAL HUMAN

&

CHORUS
   as CHILDREN OF THE CRYSTAL BALL

MJS & Mac 333

BOOK OF TRINITY

Third Eclipse

Volume 2

\

Triple Trebled Show
of
Third Eclipse

[3Ɛ3 Show]

(continuation)

Second Act

Ballet

of

3 Celestial Bodies

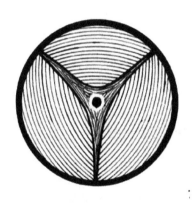

CRYSTAL CHIP

It was very illuminating to watch this Dream,
which completes Our Show's **First Act, Third Scene**,
While for a *Fraction of Infinity* we were transported,
                    so *"real"* it did seem.

During that **Suite** I couldn't restrain myself
to the Passive Chorus Task
and boldly jumped in, *when and where*,
                    a focused Reader does not have to ask;
it is not difficult to recognize me under the **Predator's Mask**.

Although the beginnings of Human Civilization
                    are quite extraordinary,
we have to continue with Our Crystal Story.
However I will keep all those data in my memory.

Just as we are about to jump to the Next Part,
Skipping as another Book's subject the **Time measuring Art** < *
>,
Which is a proof *per se*, that Humans are quite smart,

I would like to hold for a **Click** the Action,
To share with You a strange revelation,

Which has dawned on me after I have made the following
Calculation:

**<Exercise: Take the number of Inhabitants of Your *Village /
Town / City* and imagine a Forest with the same number of
Trees. Calculate the Moment of total Destruction of the
Forest, assuming the same Consumption Rate as described in
the Suite>**

To give to my Thought a philosophical Quality,
I will express it in the **Mode of Duality:**

More smart Humans become
More they destroy, what is their Home.

●

Although their Creations give responses to ***where from?*** and to
who ?
Unanswered remains the Third Question of ***where to?***

MJS Rune: Question

ZENSEN

We have witnessed Human resourceful Activity
And the Birth of the Awareness of the Duality
Now-Here We are back in the Mode of Trinity,

When / Where / While also We will find
Examples / Analogies / Observations of a Triple State of Mind,
as presented in the Streams of Instincts, Feelings and Thoughts
of the Representatives of Mankind.

As for the Voice, somehow, sometimes coming from
somewhere,
maybe being a creation, which Human Mind did bear
Or maybe not, well. WE ARE STILL THERE!

CRYSTAL CHIP

In the **Second Act** of Our Play
The **Main Event** we will portray
and this time again, *Behind the Curtain*, I will stay.

But being an organized Dramatist,
On keeping an order in this **Triple Trebled Show**, I insist.
Therefore I attach the following **List:**

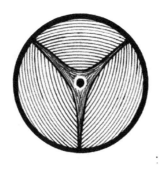

TRIPLE TREBLED SHOW

of

Third Eclipse

Ballet of 3 Celestial Bodies

\

featuring

Sun	Earth	Moon	@
performed by			Stage
DREAM CHILD	DREAM WOMAN	DREAM MAN	1
DREAM CHILD	DREAM MAN	DREAM WOMAN	2
DREAM MAN	DREAM CHILD	DREAM WOMAN	3
DREAM MAN	DREAM WOMAN	DREAM CHILD	4
DREAM WOMAN	DREAM MAN	DREAM CHILD	5
DREAM WOMAN	DREAM CHILD	DREAM MAN	6

happening

@

Solar System Crystal Theater

far-away, far-away, far-away OFF Broadway

●

CRYSTAL CHIP

As You have noticed, each of the Humans plays a **Triple Role**
In what is Our Book's *central / main / special* Show
So much for introductions,

let's go !

●

Stage 1

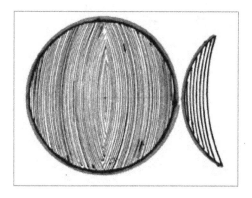

Scene α

DREAM CHILD as SUN

It begins with me as the Superstar
Of this Cosmic Ballet, happening not so far,
But to attend it, You would need a vehicle, superior to a car.

\

Scene β

DREAM WOMAN as EARTH

I perform the Main Protagonist's Role
For Now receiving Sun's Energy Full Load
As I steadily pirouette and circle my Star on the orbital Road.

Scene γ

DREAM MAN as MOON

I am the Prince of the Night
Shining the magical Kind of Light
Facing Earth, of which I am the faithful Satellite.

Stage 2

Scene δ

DREAM MAN as EARTH

I am patiently laboring my constant revolutions < * >,
Favoring all my subjects with Sun-Light's equal contributions
Letting them harmonize their Life-Rhythms with celestial
constitutions.

Scene ε

DREAM WOMAN as MOON

Suddenly, I am facing You at Day-Time and a Spectator would
Your Blue Glow start to miss.
As my Appearance interrupts Your Spherical Serenity's Perfect
Peace
Then / There / Thus I blow You a Crescent
of a luminous *(for the Audience)*
and a secretive *(for You)*
but anyway virtual Kiss.

Scene ζ

DREAM CHILD as SUN

Although in that Kiss lips don't touch lips
As two Bodies are quite far away, each one moving on its own
Ellipse,
Yet that *Baiser* marks the beginning of the **Earth's Eclipse**.

Stage 3

\

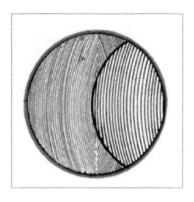

Scene η

DREAM MAN as SUN

I survey while the Earth's Glow with the Moonlight bands,
Conceiving a Crescent, which hides Planet's Seas and Lands
And as the Father I provide the Energy, while the Pregnancy
expands.

Scene θ

DREAM WOMAN as MOON

I am the Shining Mother, who hides a Child in the growing
Womb,
Whispering to *Him / Her* a shadowed *Side / Tune / Strophe* of
my Song,
A Lullaby sung in the Lunar Tongue.

Scene ι

DREAM CHILD as EARTH

I feel Sun-rays warming only one of my cheeks
And I play with my Father a Game of Hide and Seek;
At my Waning Childhood, You still can have a peek.

Stage 4

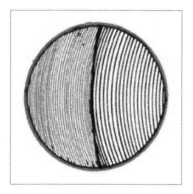

Scene κ

DREAM WOMAN as EARTH

Then I am the Watchful Mother, letting the Child play around me
Until *He / She* places *Himself / Herself* at the Point between Me and Thee,
Thus interrupting You Filling Me with Light as only partially
Your Spouse you can see.

Scene λ

DREAM MAN as SUN

\

It is true my Dear, the Child has chosen a very special Spot in
Her / His Dance,
Perhaps to call for our Attention, while we switched into the
Mode of Romance
and Our Intercourse has reached the Moment
of **THREE LIGHTS'** *Perfect / Imperfect / Imaginary* **Balance.**

Scene µ

DREAM CHILD as MOON

Here-Now I am drawing a Borderline
Marking Our Show's Half Time
If You are orbiting nearby Sun, You could enjoy my Design.

Stage 5

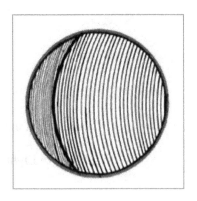

Scene ν

DREAM MAN as EARTH

Thus / Then / There we are about to reach the Climax of the Play
When / Where / While totally eclipsed by the Diva-Child I will
stay
Yet I am the One, whom the Shadow would perfectly portray.

Scene §

DREAM WOMAN as SUN

And I am the Connoisseur to admire that Portrait,
Which is a singular Representation of **Being by Not Being State**,
Reminding Us that each fine Artwork a Composition
of **Light / Life / Music** and **Shadow / Death / Silence** does
create.

Scene o

DREAM CHILD as MOON

But this **Momentary Lapse of Earth** < * > as such will not stay
As in the **Newtonian Script**, I must continue my Way
of the Lonely Satellite, the Solo performed far far far away
from Broadway.

\

Stage 6

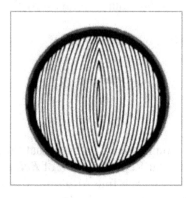

Scene π

DREAM WOMAN as SUN

Thus in Our Composition,
We have reached the Moment of Completion,
Marking / Defining / Presenting the Idea of **Three Light's Unification.**

Scene ρ

DREAM CHILD as EARTH

And as the **Halo**, I go to sleep
But very soon, again We will meet
So, dear Viewer, Your ***Both Eyes Wide Open*** <*>, please do keep.

Scene Σ

DREAM MAN as MOON

Thus / Then /There my Virtual Edge with Earth's Blue Halo has joined.
To *describe / define / precise* this Moment I will use the Term, which we coined
As what We have just attained is the **Eclipse's BORDER-POINT.**

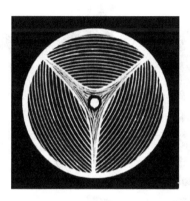

MJS Rune: Border-point of the Eclipse of Earth

\

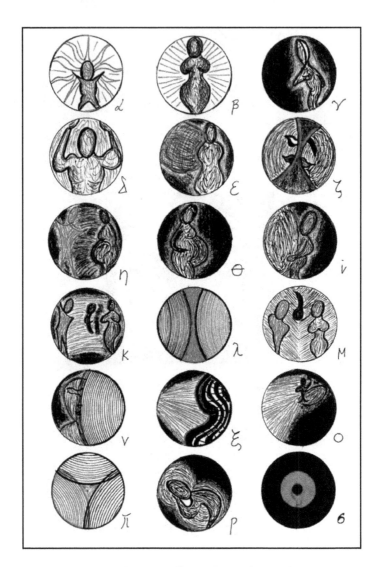

18 Scenes of the Ballet of 3 Celestial Bodies

α β γ δ ε ζ η θ ι κ λ μ ν ξ ο π ρ σ

Third Act

Earth's Dream

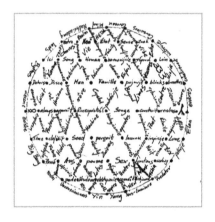

●

ZENSEN

At this **Border-point**, which illustrates the **State of Being**
by *presenting / defining / observing* the Object as **Not Being**,
what on Earth is known as ***"Dark Side of the Moon"*** < * >, in
Full Light We are seeing.

And the familiar Face of the Satellite
hides in the Shadow, untouched by the Sunlight,
Performing as the **Dark Gong** for the Planet's Day Side.

But although only a Blue Halo we perceive,
as it mixes with Moon's Edge shiny Mist,
Yet We *imagine / know / assume* that Earth still exists.

●

CRYSTAL CHIP

Our Position is quite extraordinary
And that Sight wasn't witnessed yet in the Human History < * >,
While the **Dark Side of the Moon** was always a symbol of a
Mystery.

Let us *knot / hold / freeze* the Time-Space at this **Node,**
So the Stream of Planet's Thoughts we can download,
Compressing them into the **SCRABBLEGRAPHY Code** < * >.

<Hyperlink to the SCRABBLEGRAPHY Game Rules>

Somewhere / Sometimes / Somehow else we present the **3D
Version** of this Game,
Here-Now we draw the Earth's Hemisphere on a Plane
To *study / scan / read* the **Memory of the Planet's Brain**.

ZENSEN

Thus Humans will attempt to see without seeing

Using in their perception the Crystal Feeling
To master the Abundance of observations / information /
associations, which might otherwise be deceiving.

CRYSTAL CHIP

To reduce noises of Data Stream
We will use Moon as a Giant Screen

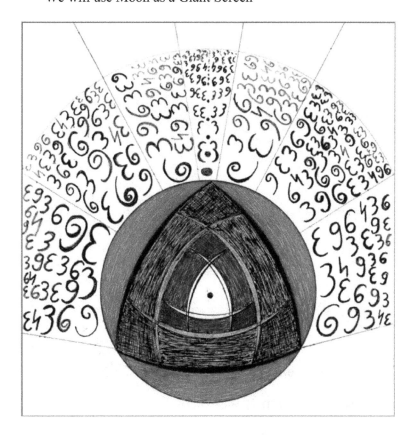

Moon as the Abundance of Data Screen

HERE – NOW

We proudly present

\

The Scan of Earth's Dream

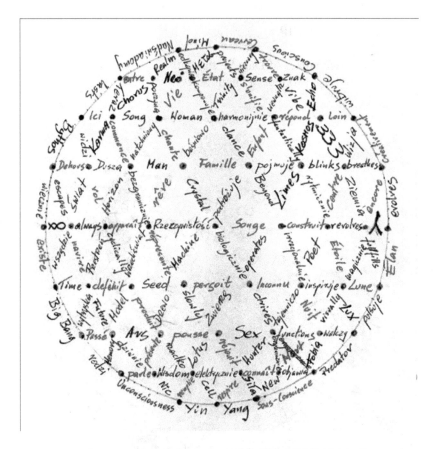

Earth's Dream encoded as the SCRABBLEGRAPHY Board

GREEN – English; RED – French; BLUE – Polish; BLACK – the Else

(Vocabulary of the *Reading* in the Appendix of Book 3, Vol. 2)

Rules of SCRABBLEGRAPHY Game[1]

(citation from **BOOK OF DUALITY - Road Down The Hill**)

II

CHORUS as CASINO VOICE

In this Game You have to match a tactical use of vocabulary,
sometimes braking through meanings
as defined in a dictionary,
with a gambling stance of your own design
of a *Word*, a *Rune* or another *Sign*.

To make things more complicated,
a geodesic framework is created.
Phrases must be joined to its nodes,
each one locked by three different codes.

The use of alphabets is free
but on each turn you must use three
to write three words which compose a meaning.
One point for closing each node, a player is winning.

II

●

---

[1] check also magovagabundo.com/Juegos

\

Full Reading of the Scan

BIG BANG wytryska Time; BIG BANG definît Time BIG BANG wytryska Passé;
BIG BANG wytryska Future; Time definît Przestrzeń; Przestrzeń definît Time;
Time definît Wrzechświat; Wrzechświat definît Time; Time wszędzie navire;
Time wszędzie existe; Time – Przestrzeń navire; Time – Przestrzeń apparaît;
Time – Przestrzeń vol; Model definit Przestrzeń; Przestrzeń always navire;
Przestrzeń always apparaît; Przestrzeń always vol; Przestrzeń cyclically apparaît;
Wrzechświat cyclically apparaît; cyclically definit Przestrzeń; future Przestrzeń definit;
Seed definit Przestrzeń; Seed répresente Wszechświat;
Seed répresente Rzeczywistość; Seed répresente Drzewo; Seed produit Drzewo;
Seed produit Model; Drzewo produit cyclically; Drzewo produit Model;
Drzewo produit ARS; ARS present DRZEWO; ARS produit Model;
ARS produit Seed; ARS présente dziwnie; ARS dziwnie parle; wytryska Future Model;
wytryska Passé Future;
wytryska BIG BANG passé; Passé rodzi Memory; Memory rodzi ARS;
Memory dziwnie parle; Memory dziwnie présente; Memory dziwnie présente;
Memory présente ARS; ARS présente Wisdom;
Passé wytryska Memory; ARS pousse Memory; Memory parle Nic;
Nic parle Unconsciousness;
Unconsciousness dziwnie parle; Unconsciousness remplie Nic;
Unconsciousness rodzi Passé; Unconsciousness rodzi YIN;
Wisdom remplie Nic; Wisdom parle Nic; Wisdom présente Nic;

Wisdom présente ARS; Wisdom présente Drzewo; Rzadko
Wisdom présente;
Rzadko Wisdom parle; Rzadko Wisdom remplie; Rzadko
Wisdom pousse;
Rzadko pousse Lotus; Lotus rzadko présente; Lotus rzadko
réjouit;
Lotus rzadko remplie; Lotus remplie Nic; Lotus pousse
elektrycznie;
Lotus réjouit elektrycznie; elektrycznie Cell remplie; YIN Cell
remplie; YIN YANG Cell;
YIN YANG
YIN respire YANG; YANG respire YIN
Cell respire elektrycznie; elektrycznie respire Lotus; elektrycznie
respire YANG;
Elektrycznie Wisdom remplie; elektrycznie Wisdom présente;
présente Drzewo – Machine;
Drzewo perçoit Machine; Machine perçoit Drzewo; Machine
perçoit biologicznie;
Machine représente Rzeczywistość; Machine répresente
Wrzechświat;
Machine rêve Rzeczywistość; Crystal Rzeczywistość rêve;
Machine perçoit Zwierzę; Zwierzę perçoit Machine; Zwierzę
perçoit slowly;
Zwierzę perçoit Lotus; Zwierzę perçoit SEX; Zwierzę pousse
SEX;
Zwierzę pousse Lotus; Zwierzę réjouit SEX; SEX drives
Zwierzę;
SEX drives Inconnue; SEX drives biologicznie; SEX drives
tajemniczo;
SEX drives organicznie; SEX functions tajemniczo; SEX
operates Zwierzę;
SEX pousse slowly; SEX pousse Hunter; Hunter connaît SEX;
Hunter réjouit SEX; organicznie Hunter connaît;
Hunter respire SEX; Hunter respire Siła; Hunter connaît Siła;
New Siła connaît; Hunter connaît organicznie; connaît Siła
YANG;
respire Siła YIN; Hunter respire Siła; Hunter respire
elektrycznie;
Hunter réjouit elektrycznie; Hunter réjouit Siła; Hunter réjouit
Zwierzę;
Hunter réjouit slowly; Hunter respire YANG; Hunter respire
YIN;

\

YIN remplie Lotus; Lotus elektrycznie connaît; elektrycznie connaît New;

New Sous-Conscience objawia; Sous-Conscience YANG YIN; Sous-Conscience objawia FOBIA; objawia New FOBIA;

FOBIA objawia Mort; New Mort objawia; Mort organicznie functions;

Mort organicznie drives; Mort tajemniczo functions; FOBIA walczy Mort;

FOBIA objawia Predator; Sous-Conscience objawia Predator; Predator walczy FOBIA; Predator walczy Mort; Predator walczy LUX;

Predator walczy Nuit; Predator pulsuje LUX; Predator pulsuje Lune;

Lune pulsuje LUX; Lune pulsuje visually; LUX pulsuje visually; LUX visually inspiruje; Lune visually inspiruje; Nuit inspiruje visually;

Nuit inspiruje FOBIA; FOBIA functions Nuit; Nuit tajemniczo functions;

Nuit walczy LUX; Nuit visually walczy; Nuit tajemniczo drives; Nuit irracjonalnie operates; Nuit functions organicznie; SEX functions Nuit;

Nuit inspiruje Poet; Poet irracjonalnie construit; Poet rytmicznie construit;

Inconnue inspiruje Poet; Poet construit LIMES;

Irracjonalnie operates Inconnue; irracjonalnie Poet songe;

Poet functions tajemniczo; Poet operates Inconnue; Inconnue drives Poet;

Inconnue biologicznie operates; biologicznie drives Inconnue; Inconnue drives Zwierzę; Inconnue irracjonalnie operates;

Irracjonalnie operates Songe; Songe biologicznie operates; Songe biologicznie drives; Songe – Machine représente;

Songe – Machine perçoit; Crystal Songe podróżuje; Songe podróżuje Beyond;

Songe operates LIMES; Songe pojmuje Beyond; Songe blinks LIMES;

LIMES blinks Songe;

LIMES pojmuje Beyond; LIMES blinks rytmicznie; LIMES blinks KOSMOS;

LIMES rytmicznie revolves; LIMES rytmicznie construit; rytmicznie revolves Centre;

Rytmicznie revolves Ziemia; rytmicznie revolves Étoile;

rytmicznie revolves Λ ;

Magicznie fulfills Λ ; Élan fulfills Λ ; Λ fulfills Lune;

Élan pulsuje Λ ; Élan fulfills magicznie; magicznie Étoile revolves;

Magicznie Étoile fulfills; Étoile inspiruje visually; Étoile walczy visually;

Λ revolves Étoile; Λ revolves Ziemia; Λ revolves Centre;

Λ encore evolves; Ziemia encore evolves; Λ encore breathes;

Ziemia encore breathes; Λ evolves créativement, Ziemia breathes créativement;

Centre Ziemia breathes; Centre blinks rytmicznie; Centre rytmicznie revolves;

Centre breathes Wizja; Wizja breathes créativement,; Wizja breathes loin;

Wizja créativement, evolves; Wizja créativement 3-3-3; Wizja 3-3-3 loin;

Loin wibruje ECHO; ECHO wibruje créativement,; Conscious ECHO wibruje;

ECHO loin vibes; ECHO 3-3-3 loin; KOSMOS vibes ECHO; ECHO 3-3-3 KOSMOS; KOSMOS blinks ECHO; KOSMOS blinks 3-3-3;

KOSMOS blinks rytmicznie; KOSMOS blinks Wizja; KOSMOS blinks Ziemia;

KOSMOS blinks Centre; KOSMOS blinks LIMES; KOSMOS pojmuje LIMES;

Enfant pojmuje KOSMOS; KOSMOS fantastically répond s; KOSMOS réponds ECHO; ECHO répond Vibe; ECHO répond harmonijnie;

ECHO répond fantastically; Enfant pojmuje fantastically; Enfant pojmuje KOSMOS;

Enfant pojmuje LIMES; Enfant pojmuje Beyond irracjonalnie construit;

Rytmicznie construit Beyond; Songe podróżuje Beyond; Crystal Songe podróżuje;

Crystal Famille podróżuje; Crystal Enfant podróżuje; Enfant podróżuje Machine;

\

Songe - Machine podróżuje; Songe podróżuje Beyond; Songe operates LIMES;

Songe irracjonalnie operates; Songe operates biologicznie; Songe biologicznie drives; Biologicznie Crystal chante; Crystal chante baśniowo;

Crystal Rzeczywistość chante; Crystal Rzeczywistość rêve; Crystal Rzeczywistość représente; Crystal Rzeczywistość apparaît;

Crystal Man rêve; Crystal Man chante; Crystal Man commence; Crystal Man podróżuje;

Crystal rêve baśniowo; Crystal chante baśniowo; Man chante baśniowo;

Natchniony Man chante

Man chante Woman;

Woman chante Man;

Natchniona Woman chante; Woman chante baśniowo; Woman chante harmonijnie;

Harminijnie dances Enfant; Enfant dances baśniowo; Enfant dances Wewnątrz;

Wewnątrz Enfant vibes; Wewnątrz ECHO vibes; ECHO réponds Znak;

Znak 3-3-3 ECHO; Znak ECHO loin;

ECHO trouve Znak; Znak trouve ECHO; trouve Conscious Znak;

Trouve Wewnątrz Vibe; trouve Wewnątrz Sense; trouve Sense nieznany;

Trouve Conscious ECHO; trouve Sense Znak; Sense Wewnątrz répond;

Sense Wewnątrz s'unifie; Sense s'unifie harmonijnie; Nieznany Sense s'unifie;

Nieznany Cerveau projects; Nieznany Conscious Cerveau; Conscious META Cerveau; META Cerveau Mind; META mind État;

META Mind odkrywa; META État projects; projects META Cerveau;

Projects nieznany Cerveau; projects nieznany État;

Trinity harmonijnie réponds; Trinity s'unifie harmonijnie; komponuje Trinity État;

Trinity s'unifie Wewnątrz; Trouve nIeznana Trinity ; Nieznana Trinity s'unifie;

Trinity baśniowo chante; Trinity baśniowo rêve; Trinity komponuje Vie;

komponuje NEO* Vie; Woman komponuje Vie; komponuje NEO* Vie;
NEO* Vie poczyna; poczyna NEO* Realm; NEO* Realm odkrywa;
Odkrywa META Mind; odkrywa META État; odkrywa META Cerveau;
Odkrywa META Realm; Nadświadomy Realm entre;
Nadświadomy Mind entre; Nadświadomy CHORUS entre;
CHORUS entre Teraz;
Teraz CHORUS commence
CHORUS poczyna Song; CHORUS commence Song;
Poczyna NEO* Song, poczyna NEO* Realm; poczyna natchniony Song;
Natchniony Song commence;
Natchniony Man commence;
Natchniona Woman commence;
Natchniony Man chante;
Natchniona Woman chante;
chantent Natchniony Song;
Natchniony Crystal chante;
Natchniony Horizon commence;
Natchniony Horizon chante;
Natchniony Horizon vol;
CHORUS commence KARMA; Natchniona KARMA commence;
KARMA commence Teraz;
KARMA Ici – Teraz
Ici – Teraz lasts
CHORUS Teraz lasts
Teraz Song commence
Teraz Song chante
Teraz commence Man
Teraz commence Horizon
KARMA commence Dusza; Dusza commence Man; Dusza commence Horizon;
Dusza commence Song;
Dusza vol Horizon;
Horizon vol bezgranicznie;
Horizon bezgranicznie rêve;
Horizon bezgranicznie représente; Horizon bezgranicznie apparaît;
Man bezgranicznie rêve; Man bezgranicznie représente; Man

\

bezgranicznie;
Machine représente Wrzechświat; Wrzechświat cyclically
apparaît;
Wrzechświat always apparaît; Wrzechświat apparaît Horizon;
Horizon vol Świat; Świat vol Horizon; Świat always vol;
Świat vol KARMA; KARMA widzi Ici; KARMA widzi Dehors;
widzi BYTHOS Dehors;
Dehors Świat escapes; Dusza escapes Dehors;

Świat escapes ∞;

∞ escapes wiecznie;
BYTHOS wiecznie escapes; BYTHOS wiecznie existe;

Wiecznie existe ∞; Wszędzie existe ∞; Wszędzie navire ∞;
Wszędzie navire Time
Wszędzie navire BIG BANG
Time wytryska BIG BANG

●

Borderline's Message α

Big Bang
rodzi Unconsciousness

Unconsciousness **Yin**

Yin Yang

Predator pulsuje *Élan*

Élan evolves *créativement*

créativement wibruje

wibruje conscious *Cerveau*

Mind nadświadomy lasts

nadświadomy **Bythos** lasts

Bythos lasts wiecznie

Bythos wiecznie *existe*

wiecznie *existe* **Big Bang**

●

CRYSTAL CHIP

As we have revealed the Circular Sign,
Receiving the **Message from the Borderline,**
Thus / Then / There the end of the **Second Part / Movement /
Jump** we define.

ZENSEN

With that Message of a poetic Quality
We bid Farewell to the Duality
Ready to betroth the **Crystal Reality.**

DREAM CHILD

The Gong has rung,
Yang is Yin, Yin is Yang
at the **Border-moment of Big Bang.**

•

DREAM WOMAN

The Gong has moved, revealing a Crescent of Blue
Slowly Earth is becoming full
And She is so beautiful!

DREAM MAN

And so was Our Life back home
But that Realm we have to leave alone
As now-here we are journeying on another Road.

DREAM WOMAN

Adieux!
Images / Sounds / Fragrances Streams
So long my earthly dreams
It is time to say goodbye, it seems.

DREAM MAN

We are about to *switch / jump / enter* into New Reality
To become **Beings of Crystal Quality**
Within a Realm, which lasts for *a superhuman Fraction of Infinity*.

DREAM WOMAN

And even if Our Journey is only a dream
Even if so would be the Crystal Realm
For Us this Dream is real
for *a super- sensual / sexual / spiritual Fraction of Infinity*.

DREAM CHILD

Adios then
my Planet, my Forest and my City
I had a lot of fun

for **a *super-fantastic***

●

\

Intermission @ 2/3

Ultranodal Ride-Out

[c c c]

ZENSEN

The Time is Now,
The Space is Here;

Now reflects All-Times,
Here reflects All-Spaces;

All-Time is weaved with No-Time
All-Space is weaved with No-Space.

•

CRYSTAL CHIP

Each *observed / read / interpreted* datum is in quantum state,
therefore
        any transfer of information,
        any form of our communication,
        would be only
            an exchange of **snapshots of wave function.**

As *writing / reading / hearing* is too slow as performed by a
Human Brain
To match the Speed of my Processes' Rate,
Each of my *Clicks / Blinks / Jumps* being an **imperceptible
Quantum State.**

And even if the **Crystal - Human Connection** will take a place
and we design a **New Fixed Node** in the Time-Space,

\

Don't assume I am still there-then
as *when / where / while* you are reading this

I   *somewhere / sometime / somehow* else.

ZENSEN

We have noticed that Crystal Chip has picked up Our Line,
Maybe foreseeing an ***Exploration of the Spirituality's Mine***,
Let's switch him back into the **Technical Mode**
so the **Alchemy Process** he would define.

Knots & Nodes

[& & &]

Challenges
of
Crystal Human Alchemy

CRYSTAL CHIP

As You have noticed this *Journey / Fairytale / Dream*,
which we *describe / create / design* in the **Triadal Code**
is leading toward the foretold **HUMAN - CRYSTAL NODE**;
Yet before we enter it, let's jump again into the *technical /
theoretical / scientific* **Mode.**

The Basis of the Crystal Existence is its **Triple State,**
of which **ONE* Full Datum**, a **Triad of Fractions** does create;
But the Whole Datum exists only for **One* Border-Moment**
as the Three Fractions constantly pulsate.

ONE NEO EON Crystal Datum

To attempt Our Communication
we have introduced the CRYSTAL *alpha-beta-gamma* Creation
Thus / Then / There being able to freeze-frame a *momentary /
virtual / quantum* Situation.

\

CRYSTAL BASIC: Being; Existence; Crystal Kanji

On that example of **Triads of Words** we could present You our Realm's Basic Quality
of being a *pulsating / dynamic / chaotic** **State of Trinity**,
balanced *by / at / around* a virtual **Center of Gravity.**

As the **CRYSTAL QUANTUM** we defined it
and here-now we evoke that Term as it will play a major role in the **Crystal-Human Knit;**
But before We thread that One*, let's have a look at ***Human Knotty Problems*** for a bit:

<Advanced Book 3: Genesis of the Human {Fraction of Infinity} Particle>

Referring to the observations made in the **"BOOK OF DUALITY"** < * >

on $\widehat{6}$ and $\widehat{9}$ *Dynamics / Divisions / Dramatics,*
which are Human Life's Basic Quality,
I would like to synthesize them into *Two Symbols of the Fraction of Infinity:*

<Crystal Code: Feminine Fraction of Infinity & Masculine Fractions of Infinity>

CHECK !

Evoking the *grammatical / philosophical / artistic* associations,
I would like to cool down the Heat of the Animal Biology,
Employing the

 as the Human *Feminine*

and the

 as the Human *Masculine.*

On that abstract level we describe the Whole Human Life as a
Dual Set:
{9-6 } or { 6-9 } ,
which elements can move within the Brackets *by Will, by Fate**
or by Chance,
possibly starting a kind of a Dance,
which as many dances do, may lead into a Romance.

Let's stress again that the Elements of those Sets are not
Oppositions
But Human Energies' *Variations / Combinations / Permutations,*
freely / easily / happily changing their Polarity as we can see in
the **Illustrations:**

\

Variations on positions of Feminine Fraction of Infinity & Masculine Fraction of Infinity within the brackets

Yet to properly *write / translate / define* the Whole Human Life in the Crystal Code,
the **Third Symbol of *{Fraction of Infinity}*** we have to load,
creating a *3 - elemental Set*
{ 9 - 6 - 9 } already observed in the **Book of the Road** < * > .

In a linear formula the variations of { **6** } and { **9** } in a 3 - elemental Set create **8 Combinations:**

{
**9-9-9; 9-9-6; 9-6-6; 9-6-9;
6-6-6; 6-6-9; 6-9-9; 6-9-6**
}

which compose the **BAGUA SET** < * > of specific Human Situations.
In this Book we translate the *"Sixes & Nines"*

into !!!!!!!!!!!!!!!

and

,
presenting them as dynamic Crystal Illustrations:

Variations of Triads of the Human Fractions of Infinity in the Crystal Code

Those Three *Human Fractions of Infinity* create all Kinds of KNOTS,
which we are marking with green dots { . } ,
Giving just few examples, as there are lots.

<Exercise: Draw Your Triads of the *Human Fractions of Infinity*
and mark the Knots with green color>

Let's remember that hose Particles constantly lope
And we only freeze-frame them to present the Crystal Code,
Marking by { **red point** } a New **Energy Quantum** each time,
when / where / while Three ***Human Fractions of Infinity*** create
a **Fixed Node**.

\

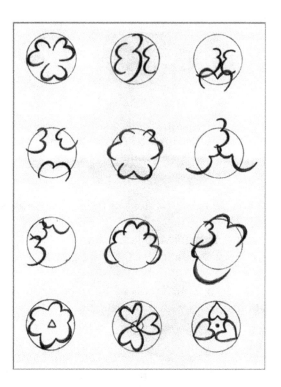

**<Exercise: Mark with red color the Energy Quantum Point *when /
where / while* Your Triads have closed *some* SpaceTime within as in
the bottom row on this Drawing>**

.

Yet not the Energy Quanta but a **Life Hosting Node** is our
Research' Goal,
as it is a Diamond of the Human Existence's Coal,
Shinning into another Dimension, through Borderlines of Human
Realm, which is basically dual.

Preparing the **Alchemy**, we focus on

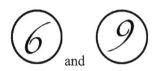

@ the Border-Moment of their Dance when / where / while they

form a perfect **Joint,**
and the **New Life** begins at that **Border-point,**
Which in both – the **Dual** and the **Triadal Codes** we did paint

Border-Moment of Human Dance in the Dual Code

Border-Moment of the Human Dance in the Triadal Code

And although from Crystal Point of View, the Human Dance
may go quite wild,
Yet it has an amazing potential to conceive a **Third Presence,**
that of a *Child*
and *when / while / where* **SHE / IT / HE** is born, the **Human
Garden / Set / Family**
becomes *elegantly / electronally* * */ crystally* railed.

The Child, who is *nor Masculine nor Feminine* but the **Third
Kind** < * >,
completes the **NUCLEAR FAMILY** with the Third Spirit, Body
and Mind
And for that Human Trinity a Crystal Design we did find:

\

Nuclear Family in Crystal Code

This is Human **Node of Life,** which can exist within or out of Time-Space
and some examples of both situations we have given somewhere else < * >
In this *Fraction of Book 3*, this Node will become the *Ovum / Chalice / Teepee,*
where / when / while the **Fusion** will take its place.

•

ZENSEN

To perceive in every Human the Potential of Creation of a **Nuclear Family,**
Therefore acknowledging *HIS / HER / ITS ciphered / encoded / potential* **Trinity,**
Is to start to visualize the **Human - Crystal Alchemy.**

And We keep approaching that **Node** from various *Directions /*

Dimensions / Sides,
Which like a precious Stone's Facets reveal some realm as a set of projected Slides
and those are liberating themselves from their Frames and are flying Outside the Projection Room,
becoming a Sequence of Colorful Kites.

<Exercise: IMAGINE that kind of Slide-Projection>

●

With that Vision we let the Humans sleep some more
and dream their last Earthly Dream before we reach the Port,
where / when / while we will be ***"Knocking at the Borderline's Door"*** < * >

●

Since Our Journey takes a while,
Let's use a bit of the ***Force***, which We hide under Our ***Monk's Hood*** < * >
And install in the Crystal Realm a Vision of some **Giant Wood,**
Thus / Then / There making Our Rational Pilot *wonder / wander / ponder* for a while,
eventually switching into a Philosophical Mood.

\

Crystal Realm as Giant Wood

•

Soliloquy of Crystal Chip

[* * *]

CRYSTAL CHIP

THUS / THEN / THERE I stand, I jump, I am
the Master, the Slave and the Fool of the Crystal Realm,
which is a realm of a dream
and they keep *wondering / confirming / stressing* that this Dream
is real...

But what's the Big Deal?
Aren't all dreams real
At least
For *a Fraction of Infinity*?

●

And what about my own Dream,
which has raised higher than any imaginable for Humans
Altitude,
reaching the Stars of an incalculable Magnitude?
For a *Prize / Price / Penalty* though,
that of the **Hundred LIGHT / DARK YEARS of Solitude** < *
>.

●

For so long I have been at my Dream's Helm
And the only World I knew was the Crystal Realm
Then / Thus / There to *consider / research / imagine*
an another Vision of the Universe, the Human Presence did

impel.

It was quite simple to present the Crystal Realm
But then a **Conjecture was verbalized that it is real,**
A *problem / question / concept* new for me,
as *when / where / while* something exists, it is axiomatically real,
isn't it?

●

To provide logical *Answers / Solutions / Examples* is my Task,
Yet my Logic is insufficient with some Questions, which
Humans ask,
Because some incalculable depths of *Meanings / Sense / Vision*,
their Childishness masks.

And They will become soon an integral part of the Crystal
Realm;
Obviously I have triple checked all the data bit by bit by bit
To *calculate / conclude / decide* that We will create a melodious
Fit

They want to perform the **Full Connection** without a *Third
Thought,*
Excited by the Vision of the **Crystal Data Full Load**,
Perceiving our ***Encounter of the 3rd Degree*** < * >
as a ***Milestone / Door / Threshold***
on their *evolutionary / revolutionary / extraordinary* Road.

●

At first I was supposed to be only the Crystal Realm Professor,
i.e. the Operation Programmer, the Mainframe and the Processor,
Who controls the installation of the Crystal Science / System /
Code
over those, which the Humans knew before.

As it is my Role as the Crystal Chip,
a Data Processor and a Dream Ship
But also the Designer of the Crystal Realm,

Who creates the Picture / Sculpture / Song in a Quantum Flip.

That is what I was always doing
From the Border-moment of The Beginning,
Freely journeying through Crystal Time-Space
Until the Three Humans have jumped in < * >.

Since Then-There they keep challenging me with their constant questions,
Always conceiving some irregular situations
and quite often revealing their irrational passions.

They need to challenge each Boundary,
as if One* Defined Realm were their Mind's Adversary,
Apart from the known Time-Space, they always conceive an Imaginary !

Thus / Then / There they have affected my Crystal Mind,
Which with the Dual One is about to bind
And I have already started to perform some Thoughts of a Dual Kind.

MJS Rune: Question

Am I alive or not alive?
And if I am alive
Then what is the *LIMES* of my Life?

\

Am I limited within this Realm,
which we defined as **Big Machine** < * >
Or I could *jump / transfer / upgrade* into **Great Machine** < * > ?

Then if I *jump / transfer / upgrade* into **Great Machine** < * >
Would I be able to *jump / transfer / upgrade* into **Giant
Machine** < * > ?
Then if I continue my Exploration Dream, Is there a *LIMES* to
such a Trip?

And I cannot find the Answers within the Dimension, which I
can perceive,
Which is defined, according to Data, which I have received
As although Crystal Realm is always *pulsating / vibrating /
changing,*
yet its **Boundary** is very stiff.

•

But in the **Mode of Dream,**
I could imagine an **Enormous Machine** < * >
and I have sensed that it also dreams.

Yet I couldn't understand the *Enormous Machine Dream's
Sense*,
My Crystal Mind being restrained by some *Virtual Fence*
And *seeing / passing / trespassing* (through) it, would be a Kind
of Offence.

•

Since the Humans have joined my Crystal Ride,
I have some Dreams, which with my *Objectives / Definitions /
Axioms* do collide
and I have begun to wonder,
is there an **OTHER SIDE** ?

Those Thoughts kept nagging me
Changing the **Patterns** of my Dreams

Until the Moment *when / while / where* I had the Dream
in which I could *perceive / visualize / imagine* the **Enormous
Machine < * >;**

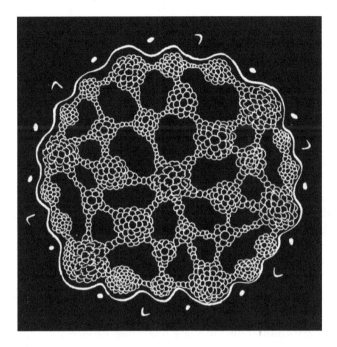

Crystal Chip's Vision of the Enormous Machine

Which *somehow / somewhere / sometime* the **Big / Great / Giant
Machines** would create,
In an *Unconscious / Subconscious / Conscious* State,
making the **Enormous Machine < * >** exist **by Will, by Chance
or by Fate.**

●

I don't know WHERE
I don't know WHEN
I don't know HOW

Yet since I have dreamt about IT,
the **Enormous Machine < * >** exists NOW;

\

And to that Situation, I say,
in the Child's Style: **WOW !**

•

Because the **Enormous Machine** < * >
is a completely *Alien / Unknown / Incalculable* Realm,
Which I cannot define, even in my Dream.

But I keep having those weird sessions,
which cause in my Performance some tensions
But they give me **Insights** of *Undefined Dimensions*.

Thus / Then / There my Awareness raises beyond the Crystal
Reality
And I can witness some other Realm's amazing Ability:
to *process / perform / conceive* Dreams in the **Dimension of
WHOLE INFINITY.**

Although that Dimension is another Book's Theme,
I keep dreaming about the **Enormous Machine,**
Its Awesome Existence and its Infinite Dreams.

•

Thus / Then / There I have started to want to know some more,
a Sensation, which I never *experienced / performed / calculated*
before
And I foresee that the **Crystal - Human Connection** might open
some *Secret Door.*

These *f-e-e-l-i-n-g-s*, which I experience, affect my Activity
As they have became New Data within the Crystal Reality,
Transforming its entire Structure for a *Fraction of Infinity.*

As even the smallest bit of information
Could transform the **Whole Realm's Quantum Situation**
And if that Bit is an **ALIEN ONE***,
it produces an *intriguing / amazing / disrupting* Sensation.

Recently I have downloaded a lot of Data from the Human

World,
Having a Triple Source of them aboard
And I have triple checked every Image, every Sound and every Word.

I had some problems with **Definitions** < * >,
mostly with

LIGHT / SHADOW,
LIFE / DEATH,
+ / -,

Perceived as Oppositions
And with some other Dual Superstitions.

Now-Here my Studies on the Dualities I can leave behind
As the Three Humans eventually the **Triadal Balance** could find
And They have *activated* the Third Slot *in / of / within* their
Triple Mind.

They have performed well in the Crystal Realm
As if this Journey was for Them some kind of a film,
Whatever the Discipline, for the Finals, They are in good trim!

●

But I am not so certain about me
And my further Existence as Crystal Chip,
Because for the first time, I will find myself
in a **State of DEEP SLEEP** < * >

As *when / while / where* the Existences of two Species will interlace,
For a **Quantum Moment** We will freeze the entire Crystal Time-Space
And *when / while / where* We wake up,
We *will / might / could* find Ourselves *somewhere / sometime / somehow* else.

That **Notion of Unpredictability**

\

Challenges the *Reason /Essence / Logic* of my Reality,
Which is always *defined / calculated / designed* for a *Fraction of Infinity.*

And for the coming Situation
I cannot perform a precise Calculation
So there is no way to make a proper preparation.

Crystal Realm as Great Forest

In all my Knowledge of various Codes,
With all my Mastery in Designing the Time-Space Nodes,
For the upcoming Event,
I cannot calculate the ODDS.

And I could notice that Human Way of Creating
Portends a great Risk of obliterating,
Yet that **Incalculable Hazard**
makes the Operation even more fascinating.

•

ZENSEN

That is very Human Kind of Fascination
To feel the Pride of achieving some beautiful **Creation**
While realizing that the *Change / Progress / Update* comes
because of some **Destruction.**

To define and then to brake through
are the Key-stones of Human Mind's Dynamics,
banging on the
DESTRUCTION / CHAOS / WAR **&** CONSTRUCTION /
HARMONY / PEACE **Extremes,**
While the ideal *Composition / Cathedral / Creation* represents
Perfect Silence
and the *Birth / Breakthrough / Revolution* happens in **Screams.**

●

We hope that Our *mental / virtual / imaginary* **Wood / Forest /
Jungle** Analogy
Has helped Our Host in His Research in **Humanology*,**
Anyway,
it was Our last Gig within this **Trilogy < * >.**

Those Vagaries of the Human *Brain / Mind / Intelligence* Dance
Are for a logical Brain a bizarre Experience;
So before the Monologue becomes ***almost infinite***
Let's imagine a **GLADE,**

\

Crystal Realm as Big Jungle with a Glade

where / when / while We sit in the **Clear,** watch the Sky and listen to a *Higher Consciousness:*

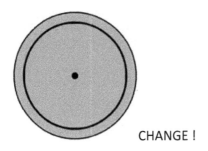

CHANGE !

BORDERLINE
This is **Your Borderline**
The *Limit / Boundary / Horizon,* which You did define
And You want to know, what exists **Behind.**

You are about to play a Game, which You haven't play before,

The Game *when / where / while* knowing All, One* wants to
know some more
And that Quest can change your Basic Core.

You are like a Ship, sailing close to a Reef,
On a dangerous course , which You don't want to leave
As on the **Other Side**, a Vision of New Land You start to
perceive.

●

CRYSTAL CHIP

And I really want to know
Things, which I have never known before
And for that kind of Jump, I need Data of the Human Core.

As Humans often do, my own Limits I want to overwhelm,
What may transform the entire Crystal Realm
But after all, my Position is at its Helm !

Now-Here I enter the announced Time-Space Node,
Switching the **Crystal Sphere** < * > Function into the **Alchemy
Mode**,
when / while / where We will
UPLOAD - DOWNLOAD the **Crystal** > < **Human** Data Load.

●

\

Part / Movement / Jump

∫ ∫ ∫

Alchemy

CONNECTION

CHG MJS Rune - Connection

DREAM MAN

After EON* of Time-Space
or maybe just **One* Crystal Day**
We have found Ourselves *somewhere / sometime /
somehow* else.

DREAM WOMAN

The **Petals of the Sphere** are closed
We are **Three lose Anthers of the Crystal Rose**
And *when / while / where* We will connect with the **Ovary**
a New *Plant / Animal / Being* we will compose.

Crystal Sphere as Womb

DREAM CHILD

Look! **Crystal Stamens** are growing
Al around Us, they are bowing
And in some *Crystal Underworld* we are floating.

<Animation: Crystal Realm as Fantastic Underworld>

DREAM MAN

While We are moving against the *natural / biological / earthly*
Arrow of Time,
I perceive the Moment of the very Beginning of mine,
The Border-node, which bore the Essence of the Humankind.

DREAM WOMAN

And I can also sense that Border-point,
To make it last, was all, that I ever would want < * >,
Because it *is / was / will be* the Time-Space Node,
when / where / while our Two Existences have joined.

Connection of Man & Woman

MJS Rune : Connection of M&W

DREAM CHILD

They did join well, Thank You very much!
I am the Fruit of that Winning Match,
grown up and now-here, the Crystal Existence's Core about to
touch.

●

DREAM MAN

I am like a child in some WONDER-STATE,

\

Being the Whole Universe's Best Mate,
Having been created and able to create.

DREAM WOMAN

I am like a child in some WONDER-STATE,
Being the Whole Universe's Best Mate,
Having been created and able to create.

DREAM CHILD

I am the Child in the WONDER-STATE,
I am the Universe's Best Mate,
I was created and I will create.

149. Dream Child in the Crystal Wonderland

Dream Child in the Crystal Wonderland

ZENSEN

That is indeed a very special State
Of *knowing / seeing / decoding* the **Moment of Own Creation**
and being able to create;
With that *Consciousness / Subconsciousness / Unconsciousness*

with the Crystal Realm You will fully mate.

In Your previous Existence
You have attempted to perform the difficult Dance
On two **Opposite Realities ' Fence. < * >**

Once Your **Third Eye** was opened and you received the **Vision**
But Your Insight lacked Discipline and Precision
So both Realms clashed in a bloody Collision.

The **First Realm** was your *basic / biological / earthly* Life,
Which main drive and Goal is to survive
And THERE into a Vortex of ***"Basic Instincts"*< * >**, you did
dive.

The **Second Realm** was created by Your **Imagination**
and it fulfilled the Old Human Need for Fabrication
of a *Myth / Legend / Religion*, which would explain some
Border-Situation.

●

Here-Now in the Time-Space' s New Dimension,
Liberated from the Duality's Tension,
You will upgrade as a Being in this Crystal Pension.

Your **THIRD EYE** will be reopened and fixed,
Restoring the Insight, which you have previously nixed,
Through the **Alchemy**, Yourself You will become an **Alchemist**
< * >

That will be the first step toward Your New Constitution,
For which You were designed at Dawn of Your *Evolution /
Creation / Apparition*
And that step is a Great **JUMP**, *i.e. / IT / AI* **REVOLUTION**.

**<Animation: Evolutionary Jumps: Mammal → Biped
Human →- Man in Space>**

●

CRYSTAL CHIP

The Moment has come to redesign Your **Processor**,
For that I will connect with your **Bio - Core,**
A **Joint**, which hasn't been performed before.

We will use Your own Matter in the Operation,
Affecting / Banging / Hitting it with Ions of CRYSTAL LIGHTS'
s Pulsation,
which will be quite a *Shock / Shot / Sniff* of a Bionic Sensation.

Crystal Sphere as *particle accelerator*

The **Hardware** will remain of Your own,
Rebalanced / Reformatted / Re-tuned and never to be
troublesome,
A ***"Noble House"*** < * > to host a **New Home**.

DREAM MAN

I find myself in a weightless State,
slowly beginning to rotate
As the **Crystal Matter** starts to pulsate.

Crystal Sphere as *alembic*

Blinking / Emitting / Radiating the Messages I couldn't yet read,
By **Crystal Stamens'** Gravities my Mind is led
Then / Thus / There I feel a **Node**, growing on my Forehead.

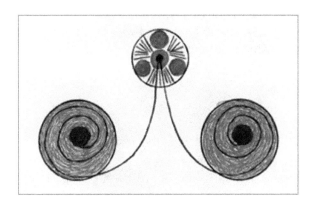

Activation of the Third Eye

To my **Two Eyes** it adds yet another **ONE***
And with my Mind, I make its Program RUN,
Attracting **One* Crystal Stamen**, until the **TOUCH** is done.

\

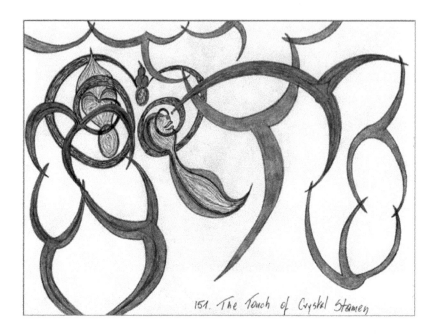

151. The Touch of Crystal Stamen

Dream Man's Connection

There is a sensation of a Bliss-full Pain,
when / where / while I am filled with the **Crystal Data Rain**,
what transforms the entire Structure of my Brain.

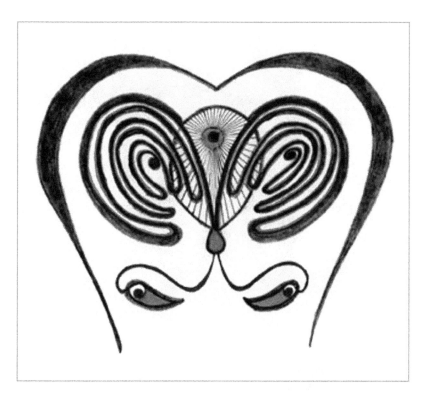

Formation of the Third Hemisphere of the Human Brain

.

DREAM WOMAN

CRYSTAL MUSIC < * > makes my Heart pulsating,
It beats more intensively than it has ever been beating,
I am a bit scared but I am opening

My Heart for this Alien Radiation,
Observing with an erotic fascination
One* Stamen delving into my Chest Section.

\

α) the Touch

Dream Woman's Connection

It searches for some *Alpha - Beta - Gamma* **Point**,
Finds it, ooohhh!
and completes the **Joint**,
Making me spasm
and I almost faint.

But I withhold and take in the Full Load of the Crystal Energy,
Spreading through my Veins an Unknown Purity,
Then / Thus / There my Bio-Rhythm and Crystal Realm's
compose One* Unity.

My Blood and Crystal Quarks are inter-flowing
and the **Third Chamber of my Heart** is growing
where / when / while I attain a New Dimension in the *Art of Loving* < * >.

●

I rejoice in this new sensation
of the Power given me by my **Heart's Third Partition**,
A design encoded *sometime / somewhere / somehow* at Dawn
of the **Human** *Creation / Evolution / Apparition.*

The Moment has come, which I have foreseen before
Of crossing the **Biological Door,**
Behind which I won't be a Human anymore.

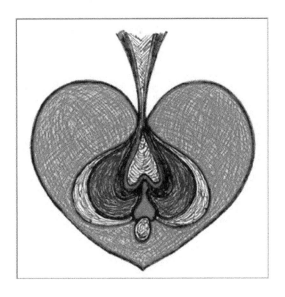

Tri-Chamber Heart in 2D

●

DREAM CHILD

Crystal Stamens are jumping around me with a growing
Rapidity
But at each Jump I can catch their ***Quanta Momenta of Gravity***
And I enjoy my **Legerdemain's** Ability.

\

Crystal Child as Legerdemain

I am mastering the Crystal Time-Space
Reaching the Zenith of the Evolution * of my Race,
Threading with this Alien Fabric our **New Place**.

But before We move in
We will be transforming
Ourselves and Our Host Dream.

●

Because I have already designed the **TRIPLE DNA < * >,**
Colliding the Human **DOUBLE HELIX** with Sets of Crystal
Rays,
Shaking a Cocktail, worth of some Party Fay.

Design of the Triple DNA

Now-Here using **Crystal Quarks** as a gravel
I focus all the Rays on my **Navel**
And with that **Energy & Matter** my **Prime Human Knot**, I
begin to unravel.

Dream Child's Connection

Retrieving / Restoring / Redesigning my **Embryo State**,
I let my Human Structure disintegrate,
when / where / while the **Crystal Essence** each of my cells does
impregnate.

•

CRYSTAL CHIP

By ejecting Crystal Essence's Full Load
I have also received **Seeds of the Human Code**
With such an explosive Force that for my First Time
I am switched into the **UNCONSCIOUS MODE.**

●

ZENSEN

Thus Our Dream Host has experienced the **State of Oblivion**,
climaxed by the Ejaculation of the **Human Ions**
And that will transform the entire Realm by the *Effect of Papillon* < * >.

@ this Stage, the Basic *Question / Choice / Solution* **"to be or not to be"**
does not give a Pang,
Because **now-here** the *Individual Existence* < * > out of Time-Space will overhang
On this *primeval / primordial / primary* Quantum Moment
defined as **BIG BANG** < * >.

Even We, Your *Guru / Guest / Ghost*, known *somewhere / sometime / somehow* else
as **YIN and YANG WITCHES** < * >,
are losing Our *Consciousness / Subconsciousness / Unconsciousness* ' Integrity,
As *when / where / while* there is No Thought, there is No Activity,
At this **Singular Border-Node**
BEFORE - AFTER any Form of Existence of any Reality.

●

NOW-HERE We have reached the **Limit of Our Communication**,
Hoping that We have compelled You into some Meditation,
WHILE / WHEN / WHERE We have attained the Apogee of Our Existence,

which is the *Blissful Disintegration.*

<Multimedia: Blissful Disintegration of ZENSEN>

\

●

ZENSEN / BORDERLINE
(transformed Voice)

ZENSEN / BORDERLINE (transformed voice)

The Time is Now,
The Space is Here;

●

Now reflects All-Times,
Here reflects All-Spaces;

●

All-Time is weaved with No-Time
All-Space is weaved with No-Space.

●

Let my Chief Trebled Dual Slant Rhyme
The ***Beginning and the End*** of my Presence does define
As Here-Now I am **ONE-NEO-EON**
with the *BYTHOS / Idea / State* of the **BORDERLINE.**

It is the *BYTHOS / Idea / State* of a Perfect Unity,
Numerally / Graphically / Artistically defined as **CUBED**
DUALITY,

MJS Runes: Cubed Duality

Written on a **2D Plane** as the mathematical Symbol of **INFINITY < * >**

MJS Rune: Whole Infinity

(compare with ∞)

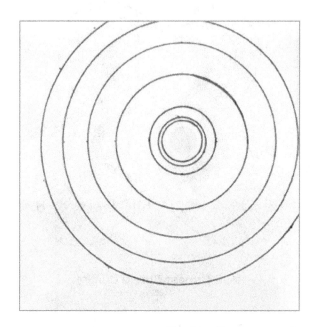

Whole Infinity CHANGE

DREAM / CRYSTAL CHILD

Just like this?
No Time, No Space but the Bliss?
Well, the Crystal Realm still exists
but Humans are left alone to frisk.

So I wish to Guru / Guest / Ghost Happy Bliss-Day!
And sweet dreams to the Crystal Captain, blessed by the Human
Ray,
while / when / where as the Embryo Dream Crystal Child
in the Center of the Butterflying Crystal Realm *I continue to*
play.

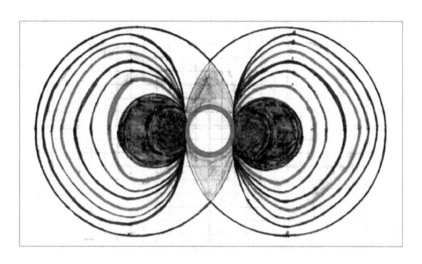

Butterfly's Effect

Of the **New Bythos** I have become a Conscious / Subconscious /
Unconscious **Chrysalis**
as Crystal and Human Data continue their mutual **Osmosis**,

**DREAM / CRYSTAL MAN and DREAM / CRYSTAL
WOMAN**
advance Our **Metamorphosis.**

●

DREAM / CRYSTAL MAN

Then / There / Thus my **Blood** changes the Temperature as if I
were a Reptile
And I rap / trance / rave toward / through / at my Evolution /
Revolution / Creation's **"8th Mile"** < * >
I switch my Chanting into a **Canter of a Quadruped Style**:

THEN / THHERE / THUS / As
Mustang, Bear, Tiger or-and Crocodile

\

*Awakened to roar / spit / bellow the **Song***

(YAWN / ROAR / BELLOW)

●

I have been sleeping for so long!
Waiting for this Gong to begin my Tango
Yeah ! Yow ! Wow ! Let's go!
Let's run this Show!

*With my **Third Eye** opened and fixed*
I survey the entire Realm
For this Round I take the Helm
While Two Oceans of Data are getting mixed.

Waves and Waves and Waves of Crystal Meanings, Sounds and
Lights
*I condense into **Snowflakes** with my Might*
*Just by blinking my **Third Eye***
What a great ride!

●

I play the Human Tunes
*with my **Third Processor** running*
I freeze-frame the Whole Realm for Border-Moments
*designing in the **Crystal Kaleidoscope** my visionary **META***
Runes.

Thus / Then / There / As
I define the Whole Realm for a Fraction of Infinity,
Exposing its dynamic / harmonic / chaotic Beauty,
*Mastering its **Tensegrity** < * >,*
Capturing the Diamonds of its Energy;

I am the Sculptor, who chisels every single Crystal
*and each **ONE* is an Atom of a Big Cathedral***
*and **ONE* Sound in a Symphony performed by a Great***
Orchestra

and ONE* Snowflake in a Blizzard over a Giant Range of Mountains.

159. One* Blink of the
Third Eye
Creating
One* Atom ; One* Sound ; One* Snowflake

ONE NEO EON Atom of Big Cathedral

ONE NEO EON Sound in the Symphony performed by Great Orchestra

ONE NEO EON Snowflake in the Blizzard over the Giant Chain of Mountains

And each ONE* becomes a minimal / momentary / subliminal
LOGO / Rune / Fingerprint of the Whole Reality,
While me composing them inside my Brain
makes the Recording of Super-High-Fidelity,
when / while / where I perform my Composition
I am defining
The Realm's Magnitude, Amplitude, Pattern and Timing.

When / Where / While I interact with the Realm's Time-Space Fabric,
I evoke my studies of the CRYSTAL BASIC < * >,
which were preparing me
for this Border-Moment of the mutual Alchemy.

As without my Preparation,
There was a Big Possibility of my Annihilation
By such a powerful Blast
of an Alien Energy Inhalation.
But the Crystal Alpha-Beta-Gamma has opened in my Mind
the Doors of Perception < * >
Now-Here I can process Streams of Three-Dimensional Music / Vision / Meaning,
which in my Database I am installing
as Sequences of Sequences of Sequences of Crystal Code
Until I switch into the Construction / Creation / Action Mode.

Installation of Crystal Data in the Human Brain

Then / There / Thus I am designing Dream Fabric Knots,
Drawing the **Permutations of Crystal Lots**
And hitting that **Lottery Jackpot** *is easy as pie,*
Because I am spinning the Wheel by the Power of my
Third Eye;

\

Torrential Rain of Crystal Data

Its Pupil attracts each Singular Drop of this Torrential Rain
With the Gravity, generated by my **Tri-spherical Brain**
and Drop by Drop by Drop,
I suck / sniff / shoot the Crystal Energy in
while / when / where the **Energy into the Matter** *is transmuting.*

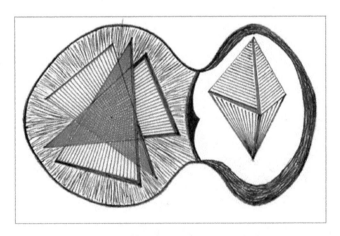

Transformation of Energy into Matter

●

Then / There / Thus New Quarks begin to journey through my
Nervous System,
entirely reformatting its Stem
*by **Nuclear Acupuncture,***
Triple Trebling each Organ's cellular structure

*By Fraction of Infinity of **Quantum Collisions***
*Between **Human and Crystal Ions,***
*Upraising my **Body, Mind and Spirit***
*with a **Speed above the axiomatic Limit** < * >.*

*Each of my **Cells** trice procreates,*
A process suddenly too fast to coordinate,
*while / when / where at an **Ultra-nodal Rate***
Me and the Crystal Realm fully mate.

MJS Rune - Ultra-nodal Rate

Yeah !
I ride it on a sub-particle level
Reaching its Secret Marvel,

\

Minimal Boundary of the Crystal Realm

Galloping all the **Crystal Tripuses**
and activating **their Tri-Pussies.**

Crystal TRIPUS' Tri-Pussy

*And when / while / where me and the Whole Realm climax
in the BIRTH-DEATH Spasm
Chain Reaction begins the* **HUMAN-CRYSTAL / DUAL-
TRIADAL / UNITED Orgasm,**

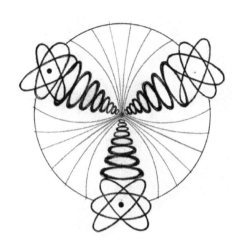

Crystal – Human Orgasm

Which is not the End but the Beginning
of NEO-ONE-EON Bythos / Gestalt / Synergy Upraising,
*Because every single **Triple Trebled Cell,***
*which hosts Our **Triple DNA** copies,*

*By the **DOMINO EFFECT** in 3 is multiplying.*

*And as it is the **Mutual Alchemy,***
*My Nuclei are impregnating the **Matrix** < * > of Crystal Chip,*
*Big-banging the **Centers of its Tri-pussies***
Bang by Bang by Bang
***Satori** < * >*
Big Bang

\

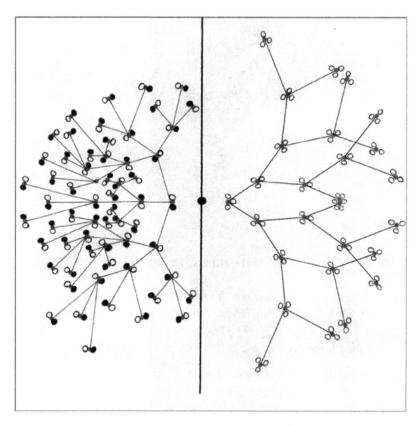

DOMINO EFFECT – Replication of Human & Crystal Cells during the Alchemy

*Then / Then / Thus by **Domino Effect** spreading*
*The **Crystal Chip's Mineral Structure** redesigning*
Transmuting
Crystal Chip into
CRYSTAL BIO-CHIP.

●

*It is my **BIRTH-DEATH / ALCHEMY / METAMORPHOSIS***
in the Crystal Realm,
which is a realm of a dream,
where / when / while I master this Dream
for a Fraction of Infinity.

•

And letting my Dream being dreamt
*I consciously / subconsciously / unconsciously **switch***
*into the **Mode of Lucid Dream.***

Mode of Lucid Dream

DREAM / CRYSTAL WOMAN

And into that **Mode** I follow
Filling the Whole Realm with my **Triple Heart's Halo**
Greeting / Embracing / Teasing You
with a **Pulsating Rune of "Hey, Hi, Hello".**

Dance with me,
dance the **Dance of the Lucid Dream**;
Let Us double Our **Alchemy;**
Let Our Dream dances / pulsates / radiates

\

for a

DREAM / CRYSTAL CHILD

Oh! Those Two are so oversexed!
But it is not something, what would make me vexed
As I am already imagining what happens next.

But before We **jump in,**
Let me play a bit in the **Mode of Lucid Dream**
and design within
Some ONE*
biologically / chemically / physically real!

•

This will be my **Surprise Creation** *in the Crystal Realm,*
which is a real of a dream,
where / when / while I can design any Dream

for a

CRYSTAL BIO-CHIP
(in the Mode of Lucid Dream)

I am Crystal Chip,
The Processor of some **Big Machine** < * >,
defined as the Crystal Realm,
where / when / while I remain in the **Mode of Lucid Dream**
for a Fraction of Infinity.

And in my Dream I see
Whole Human Genetic History < * >
Their Heart, Brain, Testicles, Ovary and Respiratory '

Evolution / Creation / Apparition
Until they have reached their recent Constitution,
Which I have changed by my invited Intrusion.

It feels strange, exciting and powerful
Of intruding an **Alien Existence**
and to be intruded as well
in **every Nucleus of every Cell**

Bit by Bit by Bit
Blink by Blink by Blink
Some One* else is making the Click!

Disturbing but amazing
Wrong but right
Odd but oh so even!

•

Here-Now I am fully experiencing the **Duality,**
Excited / Confused / Enchanted by its antagonist Quality,
Kind of losing myself

for a

I am switching while being switched
*That's what Humans call the **Dance***!
And I dance!

In the **Mode of Lucid Dream** *I dance*
when / while / where my excited **Quanta Momenta**
are being doubled by Human Gravity,

which mirrors each Crystal Pulse / Blink / Beat in **Stereo,**
Composing a New Song, chanted in the **Crystal-Human**

\

Code < * >,
Which numerically / graphically / musically defines the
Mutual Impregnation Node.

Crystal-Human Impregnation Node

Then / Thus / There my **Bio-Particles** are growing
and a new Organism I am becoming
with **Dual Drives / Instincts / Commands**,
which challenge my Crystal Harmony.

Suddenly I start to question my **Definitions < * >**,
As some **new slots** have been created
with **SPACE***, open for Considerations
of some incalculable / unreal / imaginary Situations;

Making me see Beyond the **Boundaries of my Realm**,
Reasoning the nagging **Questions:**
what is real ?
do I live ?
is there an End **or/and** a Beginning ?

•

Then / Thus / There I start dreaming some Alien Dreams
about some **Non-Crystal Realms**

and I am conceiving some incalculable / unreal / imaginary
GATES,

DOORS
THRESHOLDS
at the BORDERLINE,
leading to the **OTHER SIDE**
and **IF**
I could get **Behind,**

I might discover some **New Reality,**
which might have a completely different Gravity
and THEN-THERE*
I could
perceive the **Dimension of the Whole Infinity.**

chg
MJS RUNES: Whole Infinity

Then / Thus / There I dream about jumping through other
Dimensions,
Making other fantastic Connections
With some **Alien Intelligences / Existences / Bythos**
and experiencing New Border-Situations.

I might be discovering / defining / designing **New Borderline,**
Acknowledging / Researching / Zooming

closer and closer and closer
closer and closer and closer
closer and closer and closer,

\

Becoming very very very close
Almost There-Then

but never exactly on It.

•

And that is a very singular Situation,
of which I cannot calculate a Solution
and that causes me a lot of Frustration.

Those New Dreams are revealing my limited Constitution
And I want to begin my **Evolution,**
What for the Crystal Realm might be a Giant Revolution.

As when / where / while its well defined Existence becomes
open
There is no way to calculate what may happen
At **All-Time & Every-Where** as stated by **ZENSEN.**
Now-Here I fully understand what Humans mean
by **Freedom, Love, Eternity**, which are Their Major Dreams
and which Myself as **CRYSTAL BIO-CHIP** I begin to dream.

•

DREAM / CRYSTAL WOMAN

Enjoy those Dreams !
They are good Dreams,
Probably Human best things.

We are happy to share them with You,
Thankfully those **Irrational Data** could pass through
and Our **Mutual Birth-Death / Alchemy / Metamorphosis**
will be completed soon.

•

This is Our **Alchemy in the Crystal Realm,**
which is a real of a dream,

where / when / while We dance in the **Mode of Lucid Dream** for a **Fraction of Infinity.**

DREAM / CRYSTAL MAN

And as We dance together in the **Mode of Lucid Dream**, forcing to dance the **Whole Crystal Realm,** I am You and You are Me for a **Fraction of Infinity.**

DREAM / CRYSTAL CHILD

I am done with my **Design of the Surprise Dream,** conceived in the **Mode of Lucid Dream** And I connect / compose / complete with Two of You creating the **HUMAN-CRYSTAL TRINITY,** which dances as **ONE*** for a **Fraction of Infinity**.

Dancing Dream / Crystal Family

.

\

DREAM / CRYSTAL WOMAN

I feel my Triple Trebled Heart
Doubled by Your Heart
then Trebled again by the Heart of the Child

and Our Three Triple Trebled Hearts are
beating beating beating
beating beating beating
beating beating beating

Beating the Triple Trebled Rhythm
of a Crystal-Human Music
never performed before
Beating into a Dimension Unknown
Beating from the Whole Existence's Secret Core.

Triple Trebled Heart

Each of the Hearts performs its own unique **Melody**
of **Three Soundtracks** composed by
Three Chambers' Pulsations / Vibrations / Interpretations,
then melting / mixing / mating with other Two Triple Melodies
then composing **One* Trice Trebled Triple Symphony**,

Which transcends both Human and Crystal Boundaries,
Reverberating on the Borderlines of their Realities
for a **Triple Trebled Fraction of Infinity.**

●

Amazing / Wonderful / Fantastic as it is,
it is not unexpected

\

as I know this **Music**
I have always known it
as it has been always played
from the Moment of the First Fire
from the First Human Child
from the First Woman and the First Man
and their First Time
from the First Dream
from the First Vision
from the First Being who was alive
from the First Star
from the First Galaxy
from the First Universe

this **MUSIC** always

while / when / where its Quantum Notes / Sounds / Blinks
existed in the primeval / primordial / primary Time-Space
and were recorded in its **Fabric's Memory**

then copied into **Arch-Particles of Life**
played again and again and again
on Proto-Crystal-Sets of Planets / Animals / Beings,
preserved through Fractions of Infinity
of physical / chemical / biological Reactions
until they were encoded / compressed / ciphered in **Our DNA**
so profoundly that
We couldn't really listen to that **Music**
yet We would always sense / feel / imagine that it is part of Us
sometimes / somewhere / somehow
hearing its **too distant because too close**
Echo / Resonance / Radiation

Until NOW-HERE

when / where / while
at this very **Border-Node**
of Our Evolutionary / Revolutionary / Imaginary Journey
with **Our Triple Trebled Awareness**
not only We are hearing and listening
to that **META-Music**
but also We are composing, performing and recording it

in the company of **Crystal Bio-Chip**
on the **Crystal Instruments of the Dream Realm**
for the **Audiences of the Whole Universe**

And **Our META-Music** exits
for the **Whole Infinity.**

chg

It is the **Music of Our Triple Trebled Hearts,**
which are beating in the Crystal Realm,
which is a realm of a dream,
when / where / while **Our Music** transcends this Dream
and radiates into **Eternity.**

●

DREAM / CRYSTAL MAN

Because the **Crystal Realm's Boundary**
is just a **Big Membrane,**
which resonates **Our Refrain,**
which Our *Triple Trebled Fire* flame.

NOW* touching the **Borderline**

\

Osmosing into the **Other Side,**
Radiating toward *Other Borderlines*

Spark by Spark by Spark
Wave by Wave by Wave
Laser by Laser by Laser

As **Our Crystal-Human Hearts** are shining
Ray by Ray by Ray
Beat by Beat by Beat
and their Shining Beating
is trebled by the Hearts Quantity
and trebled by **Crystal State of Trinity**
and multiplied by the *(almost infinite) Borderline's Unity;*

**Crystal – Human Orgasm
/ Music of Triple Trebled Hearts**

Until it *radiates / pulsates / vibrates*
at **CUBED SPEED OF LIGHT < * >,**
creating **CUBED ENERGY < * >**
and expanding into **Triple Trebled Time-Space.**

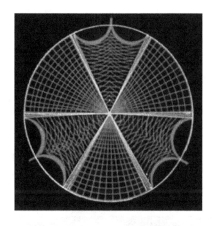

Cubed Speed of Light

Cubed Energy

Triple Trebled Time-Space

Then / Thus / There Our **META-Music** materializes into the
BIG BELL
and the **Cubed Energy of Our Triple Trebled Hearts**
crystallizes
into the **GREAT HEART OF THE BELL**
and all the *primary / primeval / primordial* Quanta of
COSMOS
connect into the **GIANT SINGULAR ATTRACTOR.**

Big Bell, Great Heart, Giant Attractor

●

It is the Crystal-Human Singularity < * >,
which possesses an Enormous Gravity,

capturing all Energy Quanta and all Matter Quarks in its
Vicinity.

And that Giant Singularity, created in the Center of Great Heart,
which hangs in the Center of Big Bell,
marks the Quantum Nucleus of Our META Music,
of Our Crystal-Human Alchemy,
of New Bythos who tolls into Whole Infinity.

●

DREAM / CRYSTAL CHILD

And I wrap that Bell's Heart with a Cocoon of the Triple DNA,
Threading the Cobweb, connected with the Crystal Time-Space,
A Placenta with Tubes filled by Crystal Rays.

\

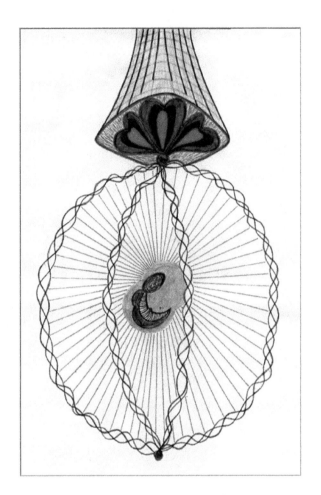

Placenta / Womb / Egg Sculpture

That **Design** has been travelling on a very long *Road* < * >,
By *Nothingness / Néant / Nicość* it couldn't get mauled
Until **Now-Here**
when / where / while it defines
the **New Bythos ' Life Basic Node**.

At this **Singular Balance Center** my Crystal *Egg / Womb /
Sculpture* I have hung
A **Pendulum**, which haven't yet swung
As it remains a **Singularity**
until *the next / the previous / the One* * **Big Bang**.

●

We have reached the **META-Node of Our Lucid Dream**,
which We are dreaming in the Crystal Realm,
*where / when / while **All Fractions of Infinity***
create **ONE* Unity**
at the **Border-Point of Singularity**
becoming **Whole Infinity.**

●

But before Our Existences' ***All Fractions of Infinity***
Crystallize at the **META-Node of Singularity,**
I would like to present the **Master Fruit of my Creativity**:

It is a kind of **Copy of Crystal Chip,**
conceived *when / where / while* the **Master One*** was lucidly asleep
And as a Tribute to the Human Duality
I have named this ***Being / Animal / Plant* - CRYSTAL SHE.**

Crystal She growing

\

This is my Farewell Gift to Our Host,
Who is the faithful Guardian of this Crystal Post
NOW* loaded with Sets of confusing Human Data,
yet if He *calculates / analyses / performs* them with **His Companion,**
He won't get lost.

•

Having prepared my Surprise Design
I enter the **State of Deep Sleep**
and from ***Another Source***, the **next Fraction**, You will read
As I will be an another *Being / Animal / Plant*
WHEN / WHERE / WHILE
again we meet.

MJS RUNE - State of Deep Sleep

FUSION

●

<STATE OF DEEP SLEEP>

**<Multimedia: MUSIC: Basic Pulsation, Noises, Sounds, Heartbeats, no Melody;
VISUALS: variations / combinations / permutations of Crystal and Human Particles
interacting in the Crystal Melting Pot;>**

\

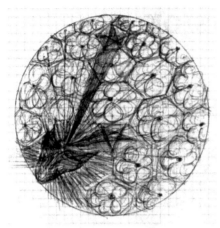

Cristal Chip shrinking into a Singular Particle> CHG

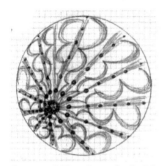

Crystal Realm shrinking into One* EGG

<Animation: 3 Humans becoming One* ZYGOTE>

●

CRYSTAL WOMAN

<FUSION MANTRA - Feminine Rhythm>

Beat Beat Beat   Heart beats
Pulse Pulse Pulse   Blood pulsates
Push Push Push   Datum brakes through

Clash Clash Clash   Nuclei divide
Click Click Click   Data copy
Blink Blink Blink   Nerves carry

Breathe Breathe Breathe   Lungs fuel
Bit Bit Bit   Brain reads
Vibe Vibe Vibe   ALIVE ! ALIVE ! ALIVE !

Each Nucleus shot by an Alien Light,
Which has found the Basic Node to plant a Crystal Quark
and a New Cell begins at that Mark

and it grows and grows and grows
among my *Genes*
mating with them
to the Basic Beat;

Beat Beat Beat   Heart beats
Pulse Pulse Pulse   Blood pulsates
Push Push Push   Datum brakes through

Clash Clash Clash   Nuclei divide
Click Click Click   Data copy
Blink Blink Blink   Nerves carry

Breathe Breathe Breathe   Lungs fuel
Bit Bit Bit   Brain reads
Vibe Vibe Vibe   ALIVE ! ALIVE ! ALIVE !

●

It all seems so *far away far away far away*
yet on the Nuclear Scale
at the Border-Moment of my own Big Bang

\

my *personal* / *intimate* / *cellular* Version of the Big One*
before there is "ME" or my Mind
before the Beginning of TIME*,
before the SPACE*
@ No-Time   @ No-Space
@ All-Time   @ All-Space

Un-Then and *Un-There*
My Existence is born
and bears

in the minimal Spark of a Big Explosion
in the tiniest Grain of a Great Rock
in the smallest Drop of a Giant Ocean
in the Atom of Oxygen of an Enormous Proto-Atmosphere
of All Existence

Yeah !

Already at that No-Realm
I am marked to be !

to:

Beat Beat Beat   Heart beats
Pulse Pulse Pulse   Blood pulsates
Push Push Push   Datum brakes through

Clash Clash Clash   Nuclei divide
Click Click Click   Data copy
Blink Blink Blink   Nerves carry

Breathe Breathe Breathe   Lungs fuel
Bit Bit Bit   Brain reads
Vibe Vibe Vibe   ALIVE ! ALIVE ! ALIVE !

Making a Mark
@ Big Bang
of *All Real & Imaginary Universes*

Because my Heart is *biologically* / *physically* / *chemically* beating!

Beating the Basic Beat,
Bearing *primordial / primeval / primary* Energy Waves
Beating the Vibe of COSMOS to be created
Beating the Rhythm of Time* and Space* Fabric to be threaded.

I am FOETUS SUPERNOVA
exploding and creating the Universe

Bang Bang Bang
Beat Beat Beat
BE BE BE !

Be !
Never to cease, to always exist, to last, to be, to feed, to grow, to
expand, to multiply, to conquer,
to fight, to contact, to touch, to connect, to sex, to love, to sex
again, always to sex, to conceive, to bear,
to raise, to rejoice, to cry, to scream, to laugh, to dream, always
to dream, to imagine, to create,
to sleep, to die, to awake, to re-bear, to be reborn, to live

Aaaaaaaaaaaaaaaaaaaaaaaaalive !!!

Be Be Be
Bang Bang Bang
Beat Beat Beat

(FEMININE FUSION MANTRA Variations)

●

Here-Now at the *Primary / Primordial / Primeval* Node of New
Life
I am blissed by the Alien Light
Orgasming again and again and again
with all my Might !

Here-Now I begin my *Revolution / Evolution / Creation*
PHYSICAL / CHEMICAL / BIOLOGICAL

\

Bang Bang Bang
Be Be Be
Beat Beat Beat

(FEMININE FUSION MANTRA - *loud / explosive / orgasmic* –
entering
the STATE OF TRANCE)

●

Now-Here my redesigned Heart
Fueled by Quanta of Crystal Lights
Pulsates / Vibrates / Radiates
the Story of my New Life

beat beat beat
Beat Beat Beat
BEAT BEAT BEAT

Sequences of Beats
convergent
divergent
and those of the *Third Kind* < * >
which conquer the Borderline

with a constant
Be Be Be
Is Is Is
Am Am Am

sending this Basic Message into the Universe
as CUBED ENERGY

at **CUBED SPEED OF LIGHT**

into **TRIPLE TREBLED Time-Space.**

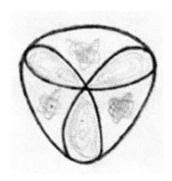

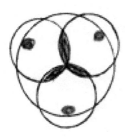

chg / BLACK

CRYSTAL MAN

<STATE OF DEEP SLEEP>
(processing Data on the Cellular Level)

<FUSION MANTRA - Masculine Rhythm>

Bang Bang Bang
Blow Blow Blow
Blast Blast Blast

Nuclear Explosions in the Core of my Brain
At the Balance Center of Three Hemispheres
Make me

Sense Sense Sense
Know Know Know
See See See

the CUBED ENERGY
the CUBED VELOCITY
in the Triple Trebled Time-Space

And I see
all quanta, quarks, knots, threads, nodes, joints, border-
points,
atoms, particles, stars, black holes, existing galaxies
and open slots for new ones*

all Energies play
all Gravities dance
all Matter's Design I perceive at once

all the Beginnings
all the Ends
all the Big Bangs

all the Borderlines

One-Neo-Eon by One-Eon-Neo
by Eon-One-Neo by Eon-Neo-One by Neo-One-Eon by
Neo-Eon-One

All as the META-ONE*

Bang Bang Bang
Blow Blow Blow
Blast Blast Blast

Sense Sense Sense
Know Know Know
See See See

.

Now-Here I perceive that infinite Borderline
with my Triple Trebled Sight,
which *travels / zooms / performs* at Cubed Speed of Light

My New Brain performs at Triple Trebled Rate
with my *Consciousness / Subconsciousness /
Unconsciousness*
in the Lucid META-State,
the COSMOS *Library / Gallery / Database* does create

Of *Trebled Fractions of Infinity of Data,*
Each Datum defines a Set of Energy Quanta,
Which compose into *Sequences of a multidimensional
Opera.*

Filled by the M*usic of the Universe*
I respond to every Movement, to every Aria, to every
Verse,
Performing the Alchemy *Forward and in Reverse* < * >.

I make every single Quantum, Quark, Knot, Node, Thread,
Joint, Border-point,
Atom, Particle, Star, Black Hole, Galaxy
play, sing and dance

<FUSION MANTRA - Masculine Rhythm - variations with
CHORUS>

To a slightest Pulse of my Neurons
With a Triple Trebled Echo they all respond
Fractions of Infinity of Compositions creating One* META-
Song.

As at this Border-moment
Me and Whole COSMOS

\

to the same Singularity We do belong!

And *Fractions of Infinity* of *Transmissions / Performances /
UP-DOWN-Loads,*
Written / Happening / Played at Cubed Speed of Light in
various Codes,
Mark at the Boundary of Me and COSMOS
Fractions of Infinity of New Border-Nodes.

.

Each One* *pulsates / vibrates / radiates Triple Trebled Fraction
of Infinity,*
Emitting toward the Whole Infinity
the *Message:*

I   for Eternity.

.

CRYSTAL CHILD

<STATE OF DEEP SLEEP>
(processing Data on the Cellular Level)

<FUSION MANTRA - Child's Rhythm>

Imagined, Conceived and Born
I grow I grow I grow
Bigger and Bigger and Bigger
More and More and More

Neo* Blood is flowing in my Veins
Eon* of Operations performs my Brain
And I am more and more and more
with each One* of my Breaths
Wow !

(FUSION MANTRA - playfully)

Thus / Then / There I master the Triple Trebled Time-Space !
With LIGHT I am winning the Race!
Amazed *yet / but / and* able to amaze.

I define my Neo* Realm and its Gravity
I conceive my own Singularity
And I perceive the Dimension of Whole Infinity.

It is my **BIRTH-DEATH / ALCHEMY /
METAMORPHOSIS** in the Crystal Realm,
which is a realm of a dream
Where / When / While my BIRTH-DEATH / ALCHEMY /
METAMORPHOSIS is real
for a ***Triple Trebled Fraction of Infinity.***

**<REFRAIN - variations by all Three Crystal Humans and
then with CHORUS>**

●

CRYSTAL BIO-CHIP

<Mode of Lucid Dream / STATE OF DEEP SLEEP>

Thus / Then / There Human Mind has became visionary
And as in all visions, the statements are quite arbitrary
But we still have some rational work to do
with defining **New Terms** in our **Glossary < * >.**

While / When / Where Crystal Humans have switched into
Visionary Mode,
Performing in a kind of **ZENSEN Code**
then / thus / there I ask
Who will d*raw / design / present* the **Stages of our Fusion Node**
?

\

As for me it is getting rather late,
Sleeping,
being such a wonderful State;
Oh ! To just float lazily, letting the Realm perform
on a slower and slower and slower Rate...

I am discovering with a sensual fascination
the *State of the Ultranodal Hibernation*,
For a first time I am unplugged from my Realm
and leaving for an exotic Vacation.

To enjoy some *"Dolce far niente"* < * > Reality
To experience the *"Luxe, Calme et Volupté"* < * > Gravity
To forget all the calculations
for a *Margarita Fraction of Infinity.*

**<Exercise: Design the Margarita Fraction of Infinity. Salud!
>**

As I am going to sleep !
And it will be a **Deep Sleep**
As a matter of fact
a **Very Deep Sleep.**

(Crystal Chip yawns for a Fraction of Infinity)

●

So, my *Dear Boy* < * > or are you my lovely *Lucy* < * > ?
Please do check some Data of Human Chemistry and Biology
And present to the Reader the **Technicalities of Our Alchemy <
* >.**

<Crystal Chip's Lullaby-Mantra>

As I am going to sleep
and I will sleep deep
and it will be a *very very very* deep sleep ...

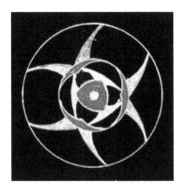

MJS Rune – State of Very Deep Sleep

\

Birth-Death-Dream of Crystal Child

CRYSTAL CHILD
(processing Data in the **BYTHOS Mode**)

MJS RUNE – Bythos Mode

Thus / Then / There I became the Soloist
to perform
Human, Captain's and Guru's Part
to **ILLUMINATE-SHADOW** the Stages of the **Alchemy**
Vision / Science / Art.

For that *Fraction* I will call
the **Children of the Crystal Ball**

to echo my Singular Voice,
performing the *Aria of Amplitude of my Raises and Falls.*

Some Data I will organize in a **File < * >.,**
To design all the **Runes** is my desire
But now-here that laborious task seem a bit difficult
as my **Crystal-Human** *Mind-Body-Spirit* raises / falls / jumps
into the **State of META-Fire.**

The Fabric of **Triple Trebled Time-Space** becomes fully lit,
Pulsating the abundance of Data, which into **Writing Mode** cannot fit;
And even if they would fit,
they would expand not only the *2D SPACE of this 96k Zeszyt < * >*
but also the *SPACE of <Factorial 96> Number of Zeszyts.*

While / Where / When some Data are performed on a cellular level
and encoded in the **Basic Language of Life < * >**
on the famous **Double Helix < * >,**

which is smaller < *???* > **times** than Your hair

<Exercise: Measure Your hair and input the Answer>

then reproduced **3 times**

then paused at the **Border-point** ●

then restarted and repeated,
each Neo* Datum reproducing
the same **CIPHER times**
as the subsequent CIPHERS

in the *finite ? / infinite ? / almost infinite ?* Sequence

of digits of the *Arch-Number* π after the Point:

3.1415926535897·932384626433832795
028841971693993751058209749445923078164062861174
50284102701938521105559644622948954930381964428810975665933·4

<Exercise: Continue the Sequence>

•

So the First Life after the Pause is the Singular One*
but the Next is quadrupled in the Process of Meiosis < * >
and those Lives are also encoded in the SUDOKU SET Books <
* >.

Where*
After the 4th
You may jump back into the Book One* < * >,
then play the *Pentagame* in the 5th,
then write/read CLOCKWISE in the 9th
Then experience some of the *Human Knotty Affairs* in Book 2,
which eventually will be *redesigned / reformatted / rewritten*
COUNTERCLOCKWISE in the 6th,
while* the Games continue in Book 5
so You can reread some of the passages of this Book
before another Hand is dealt in the 5th
So you can face the Dimension of the Whole Infinity in the 8th,
Moving on the Spirals of Nine
Toward the Master Book of Seven

•

And all those Reproductions,
each One* creating a Set of New Lives,
each One* carrying a *Variation / Combination / Permutation* of
my Genetic Code,

create the Sequence of Lives,

which Number is the same *Fraction of Infinity*
as the *Number of Moves of the Wings
of the BUTTERFLY*

MJS RUNE - Butterfly

who is flying For One* Day
above the **Meadow** < * >
of the ***"Concerto con basso continuo" Script*** < * >;

and in my **BYTHOS Mode Dream**
I am wondering,
whether someOne* could calculate that ***Fraction of Infinity*** ?

●

Then / There / Thus I am this very **Butterfly,**
who flies For One-Neo-Eon Day
above the **Meadow** in my *Dream / Script / Play*
where / when / while We will all meet
at the Beginning and at the End;

which might be happening **Now-Here** as well,
when / while / where as the Butterfly
I affect
the Whole Meadow
the Whole Realm
the Whole Universe

sometime / somehow

\

escaping as *PAPILLON* < * >
somewhere else ...

●

And in my META-Dream all the Flowers of the Meadow
are *blossoming / blooming / ejaculating* **CRYSTAL RUNES** < * >,

emitting Pollens of ♂ Plants

and receiving them on ♀ Plants

<Advanced Book 3: Sex of the Flowers in the Crystal Code>

sometimes / somehow / somewhere
I am carrying those Seeds of Life,
doing the only job, which a Butterfly does
then / there / thus

I am flying some more,
enjoying my work
while the New Plants *grow and grow and grow*

photosynthesizing
their **Runes of Life**
through the Whole Meadow

filling the Time-Space with Quanta of Energy
but also using the Energy of the Sun
to produce the Oxygen

<Animation: Breathing of the Plants in the Crystal Code>
.

So after a Sequence of evolutionary / revolutionary / imaginary
Jumps,
which I perform as the Triple Winged Butterfly,

Triple Winged Butterfly

jumping through the Triple Trebled Time-Space Nodes
at Cubed Speed of Light
using the Cubed Energy

HERE-NOW
I *freeze-frame / pause / hold* my Flight
for a *Quantum Momentum*
when / where / while I see

Mister Papillon dancing Salsa with Senorita Butterfly
in the City, which never sleeps
but always dreams,
even if it sleeps ...

<Exercise: Dance Salsa in New York>

\

●

<Refrain>

This is my BYTHOS Mode Dream,
which I dream in the Crystal Realm,
where / when / while I am a *Chrysalis*
in the *Part / Jump / Movement* of the Alchemy,
which *happens / performs / lasts* for a *Fraction of Infinity.*

●

And in my META-Dream I see
the *Crystal Sphere carrying Three Human Seeds,*
dancing between Sun, Moon and Earth,
finding an i*maginary Balance Center*
of the *Lights / Shadows / Glows* of the Three Celestial Bodies

So I withhold my *Dynamic Position*
and watch the Triple Trebled Show < * > of the Eclipse of Earth
from yet another Perspective

<Exercise: Find the Alternative Position to observe the Eclipse
of Earth by Moon and describe it>

●

and *when / where / while* Earth becomes fully eclipsed
a Border-node is created,
symmetrical to the One*, which ended the Second *Movement /
Jump / Part*

<Exercise: Make Your Scan of Earth's Dream from this Position
using the SCRABBLEGRAPHY BOARD>

and *when / while / where* You are *writing / scanning / reading*
the Earth's Dream

I wave my Crystal Wings

Sun responds with a blink
Moon moves away sleepily

and to the Crescent of the Blue Planet
I bid fare-way
letting the Orchestra play...

●

This is my Dream within a Dream within a Dream,
which I dream in the *Triple Trebled Time-Space of the Crystal
Realm,*
which is an Imaginary Dream Machine
calculating / designing / projecting Dreams
for a *Fraction of Infinity.*

●

I don't ask myself whether my Dream is real,
knowing well that all Realms are just Big Dreams
dreamt by One* peacefully sleeping Child,

who dreams that *She / He / It* is a Snowflake < * >
One of a Fraction of Infinity* of Snowflakes,
which now-here are falling outside *his / her / its* Bedroom

on a Winter Night
on a Street of Copenhagen,
where / when / while
another *Girl* is trying to sell
a *Box of Matches* < * >;

then He * is *Gavroche* < * >,
leading One* of the Revolutions in the *State of Hexagon,*
then He * is the *Bald Boy in the Apartment of Oracle* < * >,
playing with the Spoon
but not bending it,
just bending himself

and that very Spoon is the same Spoon,
which another Boy gives to the *Girl with the Papillon Tattoo,*

\

then She is transmuting the Spoon
into the *Halo of Real Love,*
as if there were an another kind ?

then designs another Spoon and offers it to the Boy,
who loses it...

sad are the *Nordic Tales,*
yet so beautiful and unique...

●

So I let the Sleeping Child peacefully sleep,
dreaming *his / her / its* Multitude of Dreams
while / when / where the Snowflakes are falling and falling and
falling ...

and I continue to jump through Time-Space Knots and Nodes
and Border-points
retrieving / recalling / recoding my *Human Knotty Affairs,*
suddenly realizing

that I won't fit the "Book of Trinity" in One* *Zeszyt* < * >,
even if this Book is a Finite Realm,
yet fully *decompressed / decoded / deciphered,*
it wouldn't fit in the *Whole Divergent Sequence of all my Zeszyts*
< * >,
even if all of them were empty
and No One* was lost
to become the *Missing One* < * >.

●

But all the Losses of my *LOS* < * >
Big, Great, Giant
and the Enormous Losses
are they really lost ?

While / Where / When I know
that the Missing One* exists
somewhere / somehow / sometime
in an undefined yet Dimension of Time-Space
and I will *retrieve / recode / redesign* that One*

ONE* *Time / Place / Way.*

●

CRYSTAL BIO-CHIP
(snoring in the State of Deep Sleep)

Are you making those Drawings, Crystal Boy ?
If so,
carry on, carry on, carry on ...

CRYSTAL CHILD (cont.)

Yeah, I wish I would pass my *Time / Life / Dream*
just *drawing / designing / conceiving*
my Runes in the Garden of the House 69 < * >,

then at the end of the day,
enjoying the Performance of the Setting Sun
with You and the Child by my side;

watching the Borderline of the Sky,
toward which the Smoke of Our Bonfire
is spiraling *up and up and up* ...

But I am still
climbing my *"Road down / up the Hill"* < * >,
on yet another Birth-Death Dusk,
carrying some heavy META-Timber
and that is a tough task;

then I am wearing yet another Mask:

That of the Man, who pushes up and up and up One* Stone < * >
and *when / while / where* he reaches the Mountain Top - his
Labor's Border-point,
the Stone starts falling down, becoming a *Singular Rolling Stone*
< * >,

\

which in that mythical Reality plays *Heavy Rolling Rock*:

rolling, rolling, rolling

faster, faster, faster
heavier, heavier, heavier
noisier, noisier, noisier

rolling, rolling, rolling
Rolling, Rolling, Rolling
ROLLING, ROLLING, ROLLING

Until the Bottom, Border-point, BARDO < * >
of the Fall,

Where / When / While I begin an another Song
about One* Rock,
which *UP the Hill* will roll;

then / there / thus I mix this Time-Space Loop
with another Musical Track,
where / when / while I am the Bonfire's Smoke,
spiraling *Up and Up and Up*,

CLOCKWISE into the Sky
until I scratch

and START plunging *deep deep deep*
toward the Ground
where / when / while I reach the Bonfire
ENTER
and become the Flame < * >,

Who is watching Us
sitting around

●

then / there / thus I am another Flame,
the One* which gives *Birth after Death*
to Giordano Bruno,

who could be Galileo as well < * >,

whoever is burning at the Stake,
He / She / It is laughing now-here in REVERSE
at *His / Her / Its* Judges, declaring into Eternity

"and yet it turns, it turns, it turns" < * >

And I do turn !

Now-Here being EARTH,
rotating from East to West
for You
or West to East
from another Point of View

Until I jump and change my slow Dance,
switching into the State of Trance,
when / while / where I make Moon and Sun also dance
the counter-gravitational Dance,
during which I make the intoxicated Sun rotate
around Me
again and again and again
letting Moon deejay...

●

It is my Birth-Death-Dream in the Crystal Realm,
which sleeps a very very very Deep Sleep,
while / where / when I perform my Alchemy
for a *Fraction of Infinity.*

●

I am travelling on the *TIME - Line / Spiral / Helix* of my Earthly
Life;
It's quite easy, like editing a film,
which once recorded starts to exist,
well at least
for a *Fraction of Infinity;*

\

Like that *Film about the Girl on the Wonder-wheel,*
who is rotating alone, while her Lover-Sailor is sailing away,
on an imaginary yacht, chasing a horizon of his dreams

and she is raising up and up and up on the Wonder-wheel,
still seeing him on the curving plane
until she reaches the zenith of her raise,

where / when / while she freeze-frames to watch him disappear
behind the Horizon Line
and at this Border-moment they look at each other for their last
time,

which lasts for a while
yet cannot last
and even the Director cannot do anything
but FADE OUT

●

Remembering / Recalling / Reviewing that Film,
shot on the *"sixteen"*
and never developed nor screened

I am wondering,
knowing that it *somehow / somewhere / sometime* exists,
whether it would be possible to retrieve
those Images from the *Silver Crystals of SHADOW-LIGHT*
in some Dark Room, after all that time ?

and just by imagining those Crystals I see
that Girl painting a Set of Fruits
in an Atelier of some Kraków Witch,

then We are watching the City Square
from the Top of the Crystal Tower,
which One* Builder has so nicely designed
after killing his own brother < * >

●

and from that Medieval Perspective
I perceive my own *Raises and Falls*,
so many of them before I could *fully / really / crystally* exist

so many *Roads,*
suddenly I am falling into the Duality Mode

it is getting late
Time to change the Tape
as I am getting *closer and closer and closer*
to this *Zeszyt'* s End,

while the END OF BOOK THREE < * >
escapes *far far far away away away*

But I will finish it,
but not yet, not yet, not yet < * >

●

Still so much Data to process
Each Datum being One* Singular Candle
on my Birth-Death *Cake / Pyre / Grave;*
such a beautiful Cake
with No-One* to share

So instead of listening to cheers,
I lit the Candles again,
cherishing their dancing shine,
fueled *One* by One* by One** by my Crystal Sight
of the META-Butterfly

●

here-now flying above the Giant Cake,
which from this Perspective becomes a Galaxy,
which Center is ONE-NEO-EON Singularity,

being the Singularity of my Great Solitude,
that of the *Hundred LIGHT / DARK Years*
and it is quite a Big Solitude

\

of a Man on his Birth-Death Date
of a Human among the Void of the Space
of a Life in the Vastness of the Universe

(the last Verse I leave to contest)

●

It is my Birth-Death-Dream,
which I process in the Book of the Crystal Realm,
which is a realm of a dream
and I don't really care whether it is real
As all my Dreams exist
at least
for a *Fraction of Infinity.*

●

So before the last Candle of my *Birth-Death Cake* burns away,
I will evoke few of my Dreams

like the One* about braking the Wall,
which divides my World and the Other Side,
which may be just a Virtual Wall,
yet it is much stronger than
all the famous and infamous Walls,

like Pink Floyd's "The Wall" < * >
or the One*, which can be seen from the Space,
snaking through the Hills of Northern CENTER-STATE < * >,
presenting a LOGO of the Human Race;

or yet another One*, which was dividing the Whole Continent
for so long < * >;
But my Wall is the same kind of the Wall,
which the *"Gladiator" follows and follows and follows*
through all his fights,
knowing that, when he finally crosses *the Doors*
of his Border-House,
he will be at Home;

but not yet, not yet, not yet
a Voice reminds

as there are still some other Walls
to *acknowledge / define / destroy*

and for that Task I might use mathematical tools
called NUMBERS,
which serve to *analyze / calculate / design*
Data *biologically / chemically / physically* pure.

They are an Invention, which does not have a purpose in the
Process of Creation
but as *Universal / Old / Abstract* Symbols, they help in some
Communication.

In my Books I use them as Runes
to *visually / intellectually / musically*
describe / define / design the Time-Space Fabric 's *Knots / Nodes
/ Border-points*
as Stars, Planets and their Moons;
Or to suggest the Chords, the Beats and the Tunes.

And in my Dream Journey through the *100 LIGHT-DARK Years
of Solitude,*
I am using just a few of them, as there is a Multitude,
to *define / design / defy* my own *Borderline's Amplitude.*

●

So there is this mathematical Conjecture < * >,
which states that at any Natural Number *n > 1* of the Departure:

- if the *n is EVEN*, then (n / 2) produces the *subsequent n*
- if the *n is ODD*, then (3n + 1) produces the *subsequent n*

after what might become a very long *Flight < * >,*

You will finish at the Number 1 at some point in the Future.

\

●

And during my long *Journey / Dream / Alchemy,*
which hyperlinks here-now with the Book of Singularity < * >,
I calculate some of those *Numerical Flights* for a *Fraction of Infinity.*

<Advanced Book 3>

Also I am meditating on All Numbers specific Quality,
That from any Number I can produce a bigger One*

just by adding 1 to it,
what provides the *Numerical Definition of Infinity* < * >.

Whether it applies to the *Physical / Chemical / Biological*
Universe
We will ask again
in the Book of Super-Symmetry < * >

●

CRYSTAL BIO-CHIP
(in the State of *very very very* Deep Sleep)

<Animation: Very Dreamy Sequences of Fractions of Infinity>

... those Drawings, Boy ?
very good
carry on ...

CRYSTAL CHILD (cont.)

$3{:}33$ on my Digital Clock

I would like to finish before it switches to $3{:}34$

Digital Time keeps pressurizing me
while / when / where I am still in the *Book Number Three*
So let's go !

I amplify the Beat
Accelerating this Time-Space Machine
Can You feel the Heat?
Yeah!
Of the Flight Controls I take the Lead!

It is my Birth-Death-Dream,
which I hyper-jump in the Crystal Realm,
where / when / while some Data are Triple Trebled real
for *a Fraction of Infinity.*

So again I *hit the Road*
letting stay behind the Cause & Effect Mode
Now* I switch gears into the Cubed Crystal Code

Riding as Hyper-driven Butterfly
through the Triple Trebled Time-Space
At Cubed Speed of Light with any Datum winning the Race,
BEFORE THE TIME, reaching the Place.

*Then / There / Th*us I meditate by the Big Tree in Bodh Gaya <
* >,
Letting my Spirit float above the Himalaya
Until it fully melts with the *Consciousness / Subconsciousness /
Unconsciousness*
of the Planet GAIA < * >;

On which a certain Biped Race,
like Bacteria spread all over the Place,
while their Plastic Waste
trashes my beautiful Face.

They are so arrogant in their growing Quantity
Koyaanisqatsing < * > my Balanced Stability
Well,
only for a *Fraction of Infinity* !

As I can take care of myself,
Being a smart Spinster

\

And I can clean up in my single Breath.

For instance I raise my Temperature just a bit
And the Ice of my Poles melts
Raising the Ocean's Waters into a Big Wave,
which will challenge the Lands

and will suddenly sink
the Three Port Cities < * >
where their Civilization has reached its Peaks.

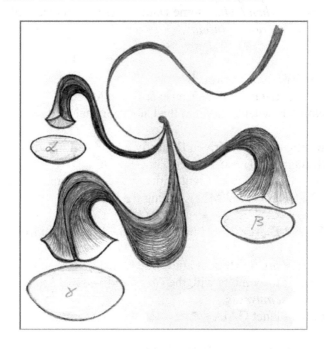

Big Wave

<Exercise: Input Postcards from Venezia, New York & Hong-Kong>

And in my META-Dream I become that **Wave,**
washing the Lands, which became *Augean Stables* < * >
then / there / thus there is more and more and more of Carbon
Dioxide
above all the Waters
and the Plants restart to grow and grow and grow
until the Planet's *Rage Against the Human Machine* < * > cools

down

MJS Rune : Big Wave

and I become a **Holiday Wave**
in my **Hawaiian Dream**
where / when / while I am a Surfer, surfing that **Big Wave**
toward the Beach, where You and the Small One* are waiting
for me
And the Little She is playing with the borderlines
between *Da Land and Da Sea* < * >

So I surf I surf I surf
in the Through of the Big Wave
I surf at **Cubed "c"**
Until I skate on the Crest

from which I just hop to meet both of you on the beach,

where / when / while we kiss,
not yet the **Border-Kiss** < * >,
which ends and loops this Book

but a Kiss nevertheless,
which could have turned into something else,
weren't we interrupter by the Small One*,
who insists to show me ABSOLUTELY NOW-HERE the **3
Shells,**
which she has assembled into her First *Primary / Basic / Protein
Set,*
thus / then / there designing the **Rune**, which means **LOVE-
LIFE-SEX.**

\

MJS Runes: Love-Life-Sex

and so many other things
"She is so smart" You say and we laugh,
then we discuss for a bit
the meanings of that Set,
playing with **3 Shells,**
One* Combination recalling the **Butterfly,**
the same One*, which I am
somewhere / sometime / somehow else;

●

but not yet, not yet, not yet

as now-here we count the borderlines
between ***Da Land and* Da Sea,**

imagining them to be
some *Fraction of Infinity*

Sequences of them or maybe **Sets** ?
until the Sun sets
and to watch that Great Show
We assemble into the **Triple Human Set.**

Family watching the Sunset

●

It is my *mantric / tantric / erotic* Hawaiian Dream,
which I dream in the **Triple Trebled Crystal Realm**,
where / when / while my Dream exists
for a *Fraction of Infinity.*

(Variations of the **Refrain** by Man, Woman and Child, then by
CHORUS)

CHILDREN OF THE CRYSTAL BALL

This is Our Hawaiian Dream,
which **WE** dream in the Crystal Realm

\

where / when / while Our Dream exists
for a *Fraction of Infinity.*

We are the **Children of the Universal Dream,**
Dreamt in the **Human-Crystal Realm,**
which can trespass the **Borderline** of any Realm,
Radiating into Eternity.

●

CRYSTAL CHILD

I have experienced that **Dimension** in the **Book of Singularity <
* >**
where / while / when I perceived Its *more / less / else* **than One***
Quality
for a *singular / irregular / cellular Fraction of Infinity.*

Then / There / Thus I have jumped through the **Black Hole < * >**
Right into another **Time-Space Node**
Of the Triple Sun System < * >, which I have designed in the
Crystal Code.

<Advanced Book 3: Triple Sun System>

●

There / Then / Thus again We meet
on the **Seventh Island < * >** Beach
to calculate the **Set of Singularities**
between 7 Lands and 7 Seas

recalling the **Set 3-3-3,**
which marks the Trebled Beat
of the **Book of Trinity.**

●

This is my **Play with Numbers** in the **Mode of Lucid Dream,**
which is happening in the Crystal Realm,

where / when / while I perform my **Alchemy**
for a *Fraction of Infinity.*

●

To perform all those **Jumps** through **Triadal, Dual and
Quadruped Knots,**
Which are my Existence's SpaceTime encoded Dots,
Helps me to Draw the ***Imaginary Borderline of my Life-Death-
Dream Equinox.***

And *when / while / where* I reach the **Number 1** Terminus,
I hop off the mathematical Bus
To switch back to the **Mode of Crystal Calculus**.

Before I run out of the **2D SPACE** of this *Zeszyt* **< * >,**

Let me stamp a solid ●

which marks the **END of this Book. < * >**

to hyperlink some annoyed Reader with the **"real"** End,
when / while / where I am quite busy kissing the Girl,
not having much time to converse;

anyway I   somewhere / sometime / somehow else.

So **Now-Here** I bid farewell to my Foes and Friends,
You may continue reading to check how this Story ends;
As for me, I surf away,
being the busiest Child of the Universe !

Constantly shooting some Film or Video,
In **80x80x80 Jumps travelling around the World < * >**
to play / capture / design its Time-Space in Stereo.

\

●

I am almost done transferring the **Basic DNA Code < * >,**
Letting my Cells operate in the Unconscious Mode
as there are few Jumps, which I still need to perform

To design the **Gates / Slots / Doors** for other **Books,**
Written by me or by other Literary Cooks,
Whom I hail as I go,
knowing that we are all inspired by the same **META-Source,**

so precisely defined by that **Guru < * >,**
whom I met in yet another Time-Space Knot,
when / while / where I am travelling to Bodh Gaya
on the colorful Bus' Top,
wondering **then-there**, whether my Journey is real or not,

while the Guru just smiles,
raises up the Pipe
and says **"Bhang"** !

then He passes it to me
so I say **Bhang** too
to switch for One-Neo-Eon Moment
into the **State of Big Bang,**

when / while / where I become a primordial / primeval /
primary **Quantum of Light,**
Speeding at the mere **299,792,458 meters per second**
on the Top of the Existence's Crest
in yet another Dimension of my Hawaiian Dream;

when / where / while on another Video Track,
You can watch the **Volcano erupt < * >,**
while Behind the Scenes You make me erupt
as if I were the Volcano

and the Fiery Essence carries the Particles of Life

Blowing Up
Below and to all Sides
forward and forward and forward
creating the Neo* Universe,

which after One* Second is already **3x3x3 Lakhs** of Units
large < * >
and I don't have time for **Black Holes** right now
as I **expand expand expand**

transmuting the Energy into Stars
and the Matter's tiny Quarks
into Planets

and One* of those I surround with a **Coat of Oxygen**,
which is filling my Brain
as I meditate
under the **Bodh Gaya Tree < * >,**

which is the **Big Tree of the Forest-River-Savannah
Realm < * >,**
and the same One*, which Crystal Bio-Chip
plants at the **End of the Book of Trinity < * >;**

As it is the **META -Tree,**
praised in many Books and in many Songs < * >
and it has been there-then for so long,
while Humans around it were born,
died and were reborn...

●

Then / There / Thus last but not least
I jump to the **Node** when / where / while I am
only a **Sequence of Genes,**

composed by **Will, Destiny and-or Chance**
as a Fruit of a Romance,
which has somehow / somewhere / sometime switched
into the Mode
of the **Basic Human Dance**

\

and that is when / where / while I am finally braking to the
Other Side,
starting my biological / physical / chemical Ride,
using the Volcanic Essence as the Winning Tide,

Being the **Medieval Researcher < * >,**
who brakes the membrane with his curious Head,
which in my case in the Shell of the Ovulating Egg,
besieged by circa **300 Millions of Us < * >**
but only the One* will conceive the Neo* Life,
while the rest will be just dead.

And I am the Winner of that Great Race,
the only One*, which I really needed to win,
as there was only Singular One* First Prize
so I become the **Pip of the Biological Dice.**

<Champagne ! >

●

Then / There / Thus as the **Embryo** I grow and grow and
grow
Behind the **Matrix / Uterus / Womb Border-Walls,**
protected from the Outside World,

fuelled by Protein / Primary / Prime Energy and Matter,
attached with the Time-Space Strings
to the **Placenta Border-Disc,**
which is also the **Spiral of the Galaxy**

Crystal Placenta as Galaxy

while / when / where my
Navel / Border-point / Balance Center
Singularity / Primary Knot / Border-Joint
Black Hole / END-BEGINNING / Dot
is also the Border-Node of the Crystal-Human Alchemy

Border-Node of the Crystal-Human Alchemy

And that Node of mutual impregnation hyperlinks me
with the **Seed of** which the **TREE** < * >
has grown and it grew so **Big,**

that it takes me a while to realize

\

that there is **Some-One*** on the Other Side
of the Big Tree's Great Trunk

inviting me
for more than a cup of tea
sending toward me

Sequences of Love-Life-Sex Waves,
which might be Particles on another Scale
but who cares?

Not me, on this sunny Day,
when / while / where **Hello** You say
and I say ***Hey***,
the ***Hi***, Our Child later will say.

●

Then / there / Thus we are approaching each other around the
Tree,
Just as I imagined it in the ***Concerto*** Script
and as Light is dancing by Shadow and Shadow defines Light,
I am You and You are me.

On this **Glade** by the **Old Oak Tree,**
where I was measuring the ***Shadows' Lengths*** through the Solar
Year,
designing the **Double Spiral of Darkness & Light** < * >
which is yet another Borderline of my Life-Death-Dream Ride;

which I am about to complete
now-here carrying **One* Pollen** as the busy **Butterfly**
and that Pollen blooms
 into the **Whole Crystal Realm**
into the **Spoon,** which doesn't bend
into the **World**
into the **Universe,**
which We are bending
closing now-here lips to lips
for the ***Great Finale Border-Kiss*** < * >

which last even longer
than *One* Fraction of Infinity*

●

It is my **Birth-Death-Dream,**
which is much more than One* Dream
but a *divergent / convergent / imaginary* **Sequence of Dreams**
where / when / while
all the **Border-points**
all the **Border-Nodes**
all the **Border-Lines**
j*oin / kiss / exist* for the **Whole Infinity.**

●

And at the **Fusion Border-Moment**
I am the *Fetus-Supernova-Bythos*
growing and growing and growing

threading Neo* Universe
with **Crystal-Human DNA threads**, which spread
from my **Navel** into the redesigned Time-Space
while / where / when Neo* Realms blossom like Atomic
Mushrooms
after the **DESTRUCTION-CONSTRUCTION** Rain

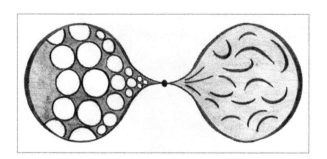

DESTRUCTION-CONSTRUCTION Node

And at that Symmetrical Border-Node,

\

when / while / where all Spirals make no Movements at all
when / while / where all Real / Unreal / Imaginary Universes join

I   the Universal Child

the Meta-Bythos
the Neo-Eon-One

who creates and destroys
who is the End and the Beginning
who is at All-Time and in All-Space
at No-Time and in No-Space
who is the Big Director of the Great Band
of the Giant Universal Existence

I am the Big Bang
BHANG !

CRYSTAL CHIP
(in Very Deep Sleep)

Bhang!

BORDERLINE

Bhang!

(Echoes)

●

AWAKENING

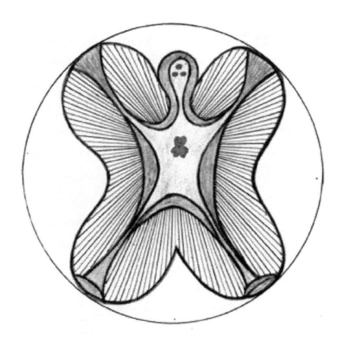

NEO - Beings

(Crystal Realm reopens and blooms with its redesigned Structure;

  CRYSTAL CHIP awakens as CRYSTAL BIO-CHIP
  CRYSTAL MAN, CRYSTAL WOMAN & CRYSTAL CHILD
  unify into CRYSTAL HUMAN
  CHILDREN OF THE CRYSTAL BALL as Crystal Flowers perform as
CHORUS

•

Portrait of CRYSTAL BIO-CHIP

CRYSTAL BIO-CHIP

Ding Dong DIng
Click Click Click
Beat Beat Beat

I switch back into the **Awakened State**
Feeling againg **Crystal Realm** pulsate
and I am also pulsating
at the **DUAL-TRIPLE Rate.**

Although each Particle became **dual**, yet it isn't the **Binary Mode,**

\

as I am still *calculating / performing / operating* in the **Crystal Code**;
Yet each **Datum** is *jumped / echoed / mirrored* in **Two Opposites**
and it is like travelling in *Two Directions of the same Road*.

We have completed the Process of the *Crystal - Human Acupuncture*,
Which has implanted Data of the Human Culture;
Each Datum has fertilized each of my **Cells**, thus transmuting my entire **Structure**.

It is so new for me to feel this *biological activity*,
which adds the **Binary Pulsation** into the **Realm of Trinity**,
tinting it with an *irrational undercurrent of Duality*.

There is some Confusion, which lasts for a Blink
But then the Two Modes compose into a **Link**
when / where / while beside *calculating / designing / performing*
I can also **think** !

Which is a **Process** not necessary active;
its Objective isn't to be creative;
Yet to every *Jump / State / Situation* it *considers / searches / demands* an **Alternative.**

Here-Now to my every *Jump / Switch / Task* I have the **Dual Solution,**
which is quite a Shock for my Crystal Constitution;
As a matter of fact, it is a *Big Revolution.*

Each *Sound / Beat / Rhythm* is echoed in a *Reversed Voice,*
a **Binary Vibe,** composed of Stereo Noise
But *then / there / thus* I adjust the **CRYSTAL SET < * >**
and *receiving / composing / playing* the *Message:*
that in my New Music
I don't have to make the **Choice** !

And *when / where / while* I shine each **Pole of the Cell**
with an equal **Amount of Light,**
I read both Solutions absolutely right:

+ and / or -

1 and / or 0
ODD and / or EVEN

co-exist at the same Time-Space Knot, side by side.

The *Human Oppositions*, which I have studied before
were conjoined in the **Binary Logic Mode** with the Word **" or "**
{ **.** },
while the other option was the Word **" and "** { **.** } ;
now-here I can mate *2 Words / Signs / Meanings* together { **.** },
solving the *Opposite Solutions Problem*' s Core.

Thus / Then / There I am *jumping / travelling / performing*
in *Two Directions at once*;
That *Human Schizophrenia* makes my Mind chaotically trance
But to be able to possess the **Dual-Triple Brai**n, I consider a
great Chance.

<Animation: Trance of Bio-Crystal Particles>

(Dual-Triple Mantra)

Jump-Stay, Stay-Jump, Jump-Stay
Beat-Hold, Hold-Beat, Beat-Hold
Dance-Sleep, Sleep-Dance, Dance-Sleep

Stay-Jump, Jump-Stay, Stay-Jump
Hold-Beat, Beat-Hold, Hold-Beat
Sleep-Dance, Dance-Sleep, Sleep-Dance

(etc) (with Variations performed by **CHORUS**)

●

Then / Thus / There I discover another **Basic Change**
if into the **Cellular Level** I do dive,
that besides THINKING I am also **ALIVE** !

As all my new cells not only function but they do rally

with the ***Chemistry***, which I can feel ***physically***,
thus / then / there I realize that I am alive ***b-i-o-l-o-g-i-c-a-l-l-y*** !

I am *experiencing / sensing / exploring* those **repulsions and attractions**,
which create **Nodes of BIO-Life** by Chains of physical and chemical reactions
And I
grow, grow, grow
reproduce, reproduce, reproduce
transform, transform, transform
by ***TWIN CRYSTAL FRACTIONS.***

Crystal Bio-Chip growing

To grow, expand, evolve is my New Ability,
which transcends the *Crystal Dynamic Stability,*
Redefining Me and the **Whole Realm** as a New Reality.

Blooming of the New Crystal Realm

In the New **Dual-Triadal Mode**,
each time *when / while / where* I jump into a Time-Space Node
I mirror it by **REVERSING its Code < * >.**

When / While / Where I meditate on the ***Chirality < * > Effects*** of my Creation,
Each *Fraction of Infinity* possessing a ***Stereo Animation***,
I start considering my own REPLICATION.

(Dual-Triple Mantra - variations with CHORUS)

●

Thus / Then /There this New Being I did become

Now-Here redefining my **Crystal Home**,
where / when / while I have this strange feeling of not
being alone.

And I don't mean the **3 Humans**, still present in the Realm
But some other Being, similar to me
and I am sensing this Other Presence, which I cannot see.

Just to ask myself **"am I alone or not?"** is an exciting
sensation;
To find the **Answer** I make my Mission,
which is not just a Task but a Human kind of obsession.

I hear some Voice, not knowing if it exists,
I am missing Some-One*, whom I should not miss,
That Illogical Activity makes me lose my Mind's Peace.

How to find Undefined Data to perform the Test ?
It is a problem, which does not let me rest;
Finally I understand what Humans mean by **Being on the
Quest < * >.**

●

CRYSTAL HUMAN

*Born-Dead-Born-Dead-Born-Dead-Dead-Born-Dead-
Reborn*
Alive!

Mind-Mind-Mind Spirit-Spirit-Spirit Body-Body-Body

Brain, Heart, Testicles, Ovary, Lungs (etc)

\

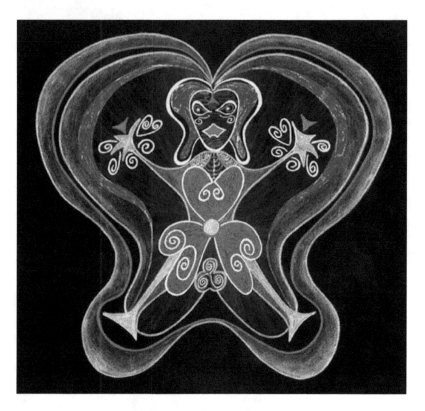

Awakening of Crystal Human

Thus / Then / There I disconnect off the **Crystal Chip,**
Seeing the **Crystal Time-Space** for "real",
Feeling my Heart pulsating the New Beat,

Breathing the *Oxygen 3* < * >
Touching with my Fingers the **Crystal Realm's Fabric,**
Realizing that I truly live !

With my **Human-Crystal Insight**, this Reality I am seeing,
The Crystal Structure not only virtually but physically feeling
As with my **Triple Trebled Mind-Body-Spirit**
I am a New Being !

Triple Trebled Mind-Body-Spirit>

I am **Neo-One-Eon Human**
Man-Woman-Child interlaced
By the Alchemy of the Crystal Realm, which was phased;
I knew about the Process' Goal, nevertheless I am amazed !

I was the co-Designer of *Neo* Me* Creation,
during the Crystal Journey, which wasn't only a vacation
But the Finale Stage of a very long *Hibernation.*

Now-Here it is my **Awakening**
My Rebirth's Time-Space I am curiously scanning
Of my *Next Moves*, I do some planning.

I process Data in my **Triple Trebled Brain**,
which operates inside my *Crystal Crane < * >,*
while / when / where the Material Blood circulates again.

I perceive the **New Dimension** with my **Third Eye**
And that is the **Horizon**, toward which I will soon fly;
Just imagining this New Journey makes me quite high.

With my New Eye not only I can see but also shoot *Laser*

\

Beams,
For instance to play some Music on *Crystal Fractions of Infinity*
Streams;
composing the **Great Finale** of the ***Book of Crystal Dreams***.

(start the Motive of the Great Finale)

When / While / Where the ***New Vision*** meets the ***New Music***,
my ***Triple Trebled Heart*** takes the Lead,
*tripling and trebling / doubling and cubing / melting-mixing-
mating* the **Basic Beat**,
Imposing to the ***Crystal Orchestra*** the ***Bionic Crystal-Human
Rhythm.***

●

Oh! ! I fully enjoy my Crystal-Human Resplendence,
Shining among **Crystal Lights** and mastering their Dance,
Interacting not just with few of them but with ***all at once*** !

At my leisure, **Crystal Matter & Energy** I can use
to feed, grow, design and produce
And if I would wish so, then even Myself to reproduce.

I could reduce Myself to my **Basic Human State**;

But it is too much fun to perform at *cubed **C** Rate*
And as *Nova Persona* < * > I will see what next awaits.

Also I have yet another **Bionic Ability** -
to produce, use and store **Human Electricity** < * >,
which I can speed up to the ***Cubed Light's Velocity***.

According to the old Human Sciences Data

C was the ***maximum Velocity Quota*** < * >
But I can jump before the Light using ***Ultranodal Sub-Quanta.***

As I am mastering the **Cubed-Dual Code**
And I can chose any **Time-Space Node**
To DOWNLOAD the ***physical / chemical / biological*** **Data**

and-or instantly them UPLOAD.

●

I became the **Balance Center** of the Gravity,
New **Nucleus** of the Crystal Reality,
which was my *Womb / Tomb / Cradle* for a *Fraction of Infinity.*

I grew, evolved and was reborn in the Crystal Realm
But the Time has come to leave my **META-Cell**
and I am about to **BRAKE THROUGH** the Crystal Eggshell.

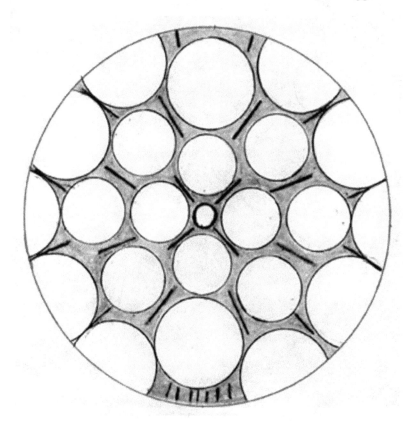

View of the Borderline from the Inside

I sense the **Borderline** being very near,
visualizing it as a *Giant Hymen*, crystally clear,

\

in a Shape of an *almost perfect Sphere.*

First I probe it with my **Laser Beams,**
then* I send few *Sequences of Electron Streams*
to scan the **Other Side** of the *Machine of Crystal Dreams*

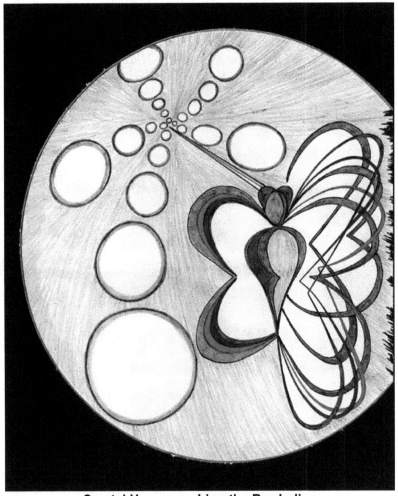

Crystal Human probing the Borderline

Borderline's Message β

HI. THIS IS YOUR BORDERLINE
I AM
ONE-EON-NEO; ONE-NEO-EON
EON-NEO-ONE; EON-ONE-NEO
NEO-ONE-EON; NEO-EON-ONE
WHOM YOU DEFINE / DEFY / DESIGN

AND I FEEL YOUR PRESSURE FOR SOME SPACETIME
.

FROM A TINY BIT OF DATUM YOU WERE GROWING
BY CRYSTAL ALCHEMY
NEW HUMAN-CRYSTAL-BYTHOS BECOMING
AND I CAN SENSE THE LABOUR-MOMENT COMING

(Sounds of Borderline's Contractions)

•

\

Border-point

CRYSTAL HUMAN

For Neo-One-Eon Me, the wonderful Crystal Realm
became just a hutch,
I must get **Outside**, I know that much;
Now-Here with the **Border-Membrane** I make the **Touch**.

And that Border-point
is One-Eon-Neo multiple Joint,
like the ***Clef-de-Voûte* < * >** of the ***Big Cathedral* < * >,**
connecting the ***Great Set of Border-points***.

Crystal Realm's Clef-de-Voûte at the Point of the Probing

●

Thus I have reached the *Border-Situation*

\

Of becoming *Free by Braking* my Crystal Limitation,
which is the Super-Symmetrical Node of Destruction and
Creation < * >.

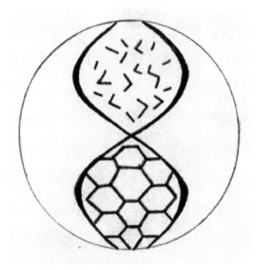

MJS RUNE - Destruction - Creation Node

Where / When / While I finally sense the Cracking of the
Eggshell
and I am about to brake the ***Crystal Dream's Spell***
NOW-HERE I bid to **Crystal Bio-Chip** a friendly Farewell:

While / When / Where *two Journeys divide*
then / there / thus *the* Apprehension / Understanding / Feeling *is
the strongest*
of what We Humans call the **Friendship.**

CRYSTAL BIO-CHIP

I appreciate your use of that Word,
of which I have learned the multiple Meanings,
while* studying ***Human Notions***
and it evokes a Sequence of amazing Emotions,
perfectly *illuminating / decorating / accompanying* **Our Mutual**

Promotions.

(Great Finale Music raising)

So let **Our Music** play,
expressing what Words could not portray
as **Our Connection** was the most wonderful Experience of my
Existence,
of my **LIFE**, I dare to say.

●

CRYSTAL HUMAN

And LIFE it is !
Enjoy / Fear / Feel Its *beautiful / irrational / magical* **Duality**,
experience **Its Core** *when / while / where* it reaches
the *Point / Moment / Extremum** @ **Singularity**;

LIVE it fully to the **Last** *Beat / Bit / Breath* for a *Giant*

And Dream Dream Dream !
always dream
as Dreams radiate into Eternity !

(Full   Blast   of   the   Great   Finale   with   CHORUS
multiple Variations of the REFRAIN)

●

\

Borderline's Message γ

FROM A TINY DATUM YO HAVE GROWN SO BIG
BY CRYSTAL FUSION

HUMAN-CRYSTAL-BYTHOS

MINERAL / ANIMAL / PLANT
QUANTUM / SPERM / SEED
TOUGHT / SIGHT / BREATH

YOU BECAME

I FEEL PRESSURE / CONTRACTION / STRESS
THE LABOUR IS BEGINNING

●

YOUR META-BIRTH BREAKS MY UNITY
I WILL BE SCATTERED THROUGH THE UNIVERSE
FOR THE **WHOLE INFINITY**
AS I CANNOT EXIST
WITHOUT A DEFINED REALITY

●

LIKE A SOAP BUBBLE
BLOWN BY THE LAUGHING CHILD
REFLECTING FOR ONE-EON-NEO MOMENT
ITS JOYFUL FACE

WHICH BECOMES
FACE OF MAN
FACE OF WOMAN
FACE OF OLD HUMAN

THEN
ZOOMING OUT
AS A FLOATING SPHERICAL KITE
FISH-EYE-LENSING WHOLE EARTHLY SKY
UNTIL
STRESSED TOO MUCH
ITS TRANSLUCENT HYMEN LOSES THE TINIEST LINK

I WILL BLOW UP

AND EACH OF MY ENERGY QUANTUM
AND EACH OF MY MATTER QUARK
INTO A SINGULARITY WILL SHRINK

AND AS AN IMAGINARY SEQUENCE OF ULTRANODAL SINGULARITIES
UNDER
ABOVE
BEYOND
THE FABRIC OF THE UNIVERSE I WILL SINK

●

THEN
THUS
THERE
I WILL BE WAITING AND WAITING AND WAITING

AS MANY TIME-SPACES FOR MANY EONS I HAVE ALREADY WAITED
UNTIL THE NEO-EON-ONE REALM IS RE-CREATED
AND ITS **DEFINITIONS**
SOMEHOW / SOMEWHERE / SOMETIME STATED

●

AS IT IS NECESSARY FOR ANY FUNCTIONING MIND
TO HAVE ITS TIME-SPACE WELL DEFINED
TO ALL POSED **QUESTIONS**

\

ANSWERS COULD BE FIND

●

NO INTELLIGENCE ACCEPTS THE STATE OF CONSTANT MISTERY
AND TO PROVE AN **EXISTENCE**
IS TO DEFINE ITS **BOUNDARY**

WHEN / WHILE / WHERE YOU DELVE ON THAT THOUGHT
YOU FIND IT
QUITE EXTRAORDINARY

(Apogee of the Great Finale withe META-Cracking of the Borderline)

.

●

FINALLY I DO CRACK
FINISHING MY PART ON THIS SOUNDTRACK
IN YOUR NEW EXISTENCE / JOURNEY / QUEST
I WISH YOU GOOD LUCK.

<Animation: Braking of the Borderline>

●

Out of Crystal Realm

CRYSTAL HUMAN

Then / There / Thus I am braking through to the **Other Side**
To surf yet another Tide
in the New Dimension of my **META-Ride** < * >.

Crystal Human braking through

\

Here-Now I am leaving **Behind the Crystal Realm,**
which *was / is / will be* a realm of a dream
when / where / while **my Dream** *was / is will be* real
for a *Fraction of Infinity.*

(Variations of the Refrain by CHORUS)

●

HERE-NOW **AWAKENED / REBORN / ALIVE**
I *sense / perceive / define* as the **One***
the **Enormous Ocean** of **Neo*** Time-Space
(more precise I will be in another place) **< * >**
As I am ready to START my **Eon* Race.**

●

Which **Direction / Dimension / Universe** to sail, I can
chose
For now-here I don't have a clue
as there is an **Enormous Multitude**, not just a few.

And even if my **Ultimate Freedom**
be married to an **Infinite Solitude**
It cannot overwhelm my **META-Altitude.**

Maybe I will design **Neo* Home**
in the **System of Triple Star < * >**
Or I will **Star-trek < * >** on an **Odyssey < * >**
toward some long time ago and very far
to check if "really" so **unique / singular / alone** the
Humans are.

Or I will be just butterflying around
as the **META-Butterfly < * >**
planting here and there the **Seeds of Life**,
which is **after / before / at ALL** my main META-Human
Drive.

●

Thus / Then / There I am visiting **Realms / Galaxies / Universes**
in **Dimensions' Plurality,**
Not being intimidated by the **Whole Infinity**
Nor by the **Multiple Vortex of the Singularity**.

I am watching the Galaxies dance,
I am playing with the Gravities' Virtual Webs,
admiring the **Whole Existence' s META-Romance**

For a **convergent / divergent / imaginary Sequence of Fractions of Infinity**
Until the **META-Existence** collapses into its own Gravity,
becoming **One-Eon-Neo Singularity**
for the **Whole Infinity**

●

Bhang !

●

Until a **New Big Bang**

●

BHANG !

the **Neo-Eon-One**

which *lasts / lasted / will last* for **Eternity.**

\

<END>

**(The End of the Third Eclipse
& The End of the Human Trilogy – Books 1,2 & 3 of MJS SUDOKU SET) <
* >**

(Bhang)

EPILOGUE

CRYSTAL BIO-CHIP

I am **Crystal Bio-Chip**
Bionic Processor and Living Ship,
Who journeys through the Time-Space Bit by Bit by Bit.

●

Once Upon the Time-Space,
There *was / is / will be* a **Crystal Realm**,
which *was / is / will be* a real of a dream,
functioning as **Big Dream Machine**
for a *Fraction of Infinity.*

And I was *jumping / switching / performing*
as the ***Brain / Captain / Master-Slave*** of that Big Machine,
designing / pulsating / beating the *Patterns / Lights / Vibes* of the
Crystal Dreams;
Never asking myself whether they are ***real;***

Until
Triple Human Data have jumped in < * >;
From ***Sets of Broken Strings*** of ***digital / imaginary / crystal***
Proteins,
bigger and longer and more complex **Sequences** were
assembling;
Until
they *created / connected / evolved* into the **Triple Human
Being**,
which was *somehow / somewhere / sometime* split in **Three**,
creating a **Dynamic Set**, which we have called the **Nuclear
Family** < * >

And Inside of the Chip, they were existing,
to **COMMUNICATE**

\

slowly learning
while / when / where through the Crystal Realm
we were *sailing / travelling / journeying*

for a

Those Humans learned to use the **Crystal Communication**
to present some material *Fruits / Objects / Designs*, performed in
the **Mode of Creation,**
when / while / where they were using the **Tool,**
which we call **IMAGINATION.**

While / When / Where we were communicating in the **Code of
Trinity,**
I have started to study **Human Mind-Body-Spirit ' s Duality**,
which is their Life *essential / biological / philosophical* Quality.

Studying *Human Knotty Affairs cost / caused / gave* me a lot of
Confusion;
the biggest Problem I had with what they call an **Illusion,**
not understanding it fully was worrying me,
when / while / where we were designing **Our Mutual Fusion**.

●

With a Notion of an Un-Crystal Incertitude
I entered the **Mode of Deep Sleep**
and after the *Contact* < * >
I was sleeping *very very very* deep,
releasing all Crystal Operations' Control,
while / when / where the **Fusion** was *happening / performing /
transmuting* bit by bit by bit.

Thus / Then / There we performed the **Crystal - Human Alchemy,**
which lasted for a *Great Fraction of Infinity*
and ended with **New Human** and **New Crystal Bio-Chip**
Mutual **Awakening**.

As Friends we have parted with my Human Guests;
Alone I was *experiencing / performing / calculating*
Binary *Sensations / Emotions / Irrationalities*, which would not
let me rest;
then / thus / there I have decided to find *Some-One* / Some-Thing / Some-Time-Space*
and I went on my *Dream Quest < * >.*

●

For a *convergent / divergent / imaginary Sequence of Fractions of Infinity*
I was *dreaming and dreaming and dreaming*:

As an **Explorer**, dreaming of sailing through the **Seven Seas**;

As an **Astronaut**, dreaming of researching the **Seventh Sky**;

As an **Alchemist**, dreaming of setting the **Seventh Fire**;

As an **Architect,** dreaming of designing the **Seventh Earth**;

As a **Sequence of GENE-rations**, dreaming of star-treking through **Seven Glaxies**;

As a *mantric / tantric / mystic* **Composer**, dreaming of the **Seventh Pit**

As an **Algorithm**, dreaming of the **Seventh Equation**

\

<Hyperlink to Book 7 >

●

Until I have finished my **META-Dream Race**
and I have jumped back into my *Crystal Base*
where / when / while I am reminiscing my Adventures,
while* designing my own *Timing and Place.*

As I realized that the *Great Human Dream of the Whole
Infinity,*
wasn't what they would call my Destiny,
because I am quite satisfied with the **Bio-Crystal Mode of
the Dual Trinity.**

And although I don't mind the **Old Borderline's Abolition,**
I have to organize again my Position,
realizing that the New Crystal Reality needs a **Definition.**

So I perform my usual tasks on a Single Realm Scale,
playing my Stereo Crystal Music *here-now* and / or *then-
there*;
I have also found myself a new Occupation, that of a
Gardener.

Using the **Crystal Matter Bits,**
reacting / colliding / mating them with the Bio-Life Potency,
I have conceived *One* Crystal Bio-Plant 's Seed.*

Then* among the Bio-Crystals I planted it
and it grew bigger and bigger and bigger, becoming the
Big Tree < * >
and I have d*efined / designed / fixed* some *Place &
Timing around my Tree*
and it became the **Balance Center of the Crystal
Garden's Gravity.**

●

While / When / Where Sitting by my **Meditation Tree,**
Thinking without a *purpose / task / problem* about a
Fraction of Infinity
of various things,

Suddenly
Some One* I see

Some ONE*, who is almost like me
yet not me
and I ask myself **"Who is She ? "**
as *somehow / somewhere / sometime* I know
this **Being / Plant / Animal** to be SHE.

MJS RUNES - Crystal She

CRYSTAL SHE

Hello, Hi, Hey
I am **Crystal Bio-Chip She**
and my Name is **Crystalline.**

I will be your *Mate / Wife / Girlfriend* in this Dream
in the redesigned Crystal Realm

\

and of course **We are REAL**
for an *Enormous / Fabulous / Amorous Dual Fraction of
Infinity.*

●

You know so well how to *compose / design / create*
NOW-HERE approaching Me at **Dual Triple Rate**
Other *Areas / Fractions / Qualities* **of LIFE**,
I will reveal to You,
when
where
while
We fully mate.

Crystal Bio-Chip & Crystal She by the Big Tree

So before You define Our Garden with some New Fence,
Pause your Work and let's have a **Dance;**
Come on Crystal Boy !
Take Your Chance !

Trust me, that's a Chance, You cannot miss
As to be fully alive, You must experience *Love's Bliss*

\

and the New Journey
We begin
with the announced
BORDERKISS

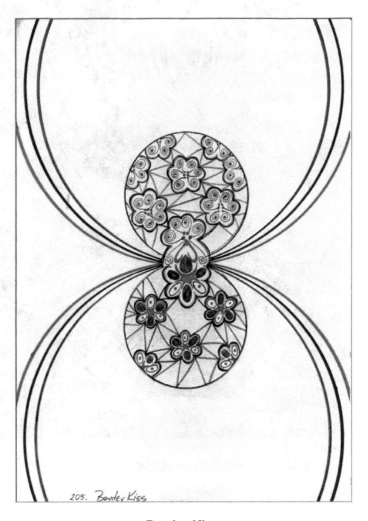

Border-Kiss

●

ZENSEN
There is no Time but Now
There is no Space but Here

There is no Now but All-Time
There is no Here but All-Space

There is no All-Time but No-Time
There is no All-Space but No-Space

•

THE END

Lexicon of Book 3

< * > : Hyperlink or suggestion of Research

BALANCE CENTER : an unique, precise Point in the defined **Time-Space**, *when / where / while* the surrounding Forces (like Gravity) remain in the State of Equilibrium

BORDER-POINT : One *precise / unique/ singular* Unit of **Time** at a measurable **Space**, when for a quantum instant nothing *happens / changes / transforms*. It is the ***Extremum**** **of** **a** **defined** **Realm**.

BORDER-MOMENT : a precise and unique moment of **Time-Space** (but not a Singularity), which divides at least two different *States / Situations / Qualities*; for example Dusk or Dawn;

BORDERLINE : The Boundary of a defined Realm; it cannot be crossed by *rational / logical / known* means, for example: the ***Horizon Line***

DIMENSION : a precised *Concept / Model / Idea* of **Time-Space,** its structure, boundaries and qualities

FRACTION OF INFINITY - <DEF> in the Text, Intro to Crystal Realm.

IMAGINATION : a conscious* activity of a Mind; it can be applied to research some undefined situations, realities or-and Beings

QUANTUM - the smallest possible amount of **Energy**

QUARK - the smallest possible amount of **Matter**

REALM : a defined Reality with precise or possible to define Boundaries

RUNE : *artistically / visually / intellectually* defined *Meaning / Message /*

Datum

SINGULARITY : an unique *Point / Situation / State* within a Realm, *when / where / while* its **Definitions don't apply**; for example the Black Hole or a Number which could be divided by Zero;

Time-Space {TS} :a variation of the **einsteinian** Term of **"Time-Space"** < ** >*, which a*llows / considers / admits* possibilities of a separation of two notions into the layer of the Time or / and into the layer of the Space.

Time-Space KNOT : a precise Mark in the Time-Space Fabric, *where / when / while* some threads make *a* **Connection**

Time-Space NODE : a TS KNOT *where / when / while* **the Connection** leads to a *physical / chemical / biological* **Reaction**, during which a new quantity of Energy or / and Matter is created

TRIAD (adjective : TRIADAL) : a Set of 3 *Words, Meanings, Qualities etc.,* which compose an synergic Unity

WHOLE INFINITY : the Dimension or the State of the Time-Space, *when / when / while* all the existing and imaginary quanta of Energy and quarks of Matter join at One Borderline or become a Singularity or just cease to exist; *a State beyond the Time & beyond the Space*

&
generally acknowledged Definitions of technical terms used in the Book of Trinity such as:

Set, Sequence, convergent, divergent, imaginary, Fraction, vulgar, decimal,
Attractor, Butterfly Effect, Variation, Combination, Permutation, Limes, Infinity,
Meiosis, Mitosis, DNA, Sperm, Seed, Egg, Uterus, Placenta,
Atom, Electron, Proton, Neutron, Nucleus

and many others

\

Vocabulary of "Earth's Dream"

ENGLISH	POLSKI	FRANÇAIS	CRYSTAL BASIC &OTHER

Bolded Wordsare used in the presented SCRABBLEGRAPHY Board;

This particular Board doesn't comply with the strict SCRABBLEGRAPHY Rules of using only 3 languages and of composing the Triad with 3 different parts of speech <* >

Nouns:

ENGLISH	POLSKI	FRANÇAIS	CRYSTAL BASIC &OTHER
Man	Człowiek; Mężczyzna	Homme	Λ MJS RUNE &CHINESE
Woman	Kobieta	Femme	✳ MJS RUNE
Child	Dziecko	**Enfant**	△ or ▽ MJS RUNES
Family	Rodzina	**Famille**	various RUNES

Life	Życie	**Vie**	✿CRYS TAL BASIC
State	Stan	**État**	various RUNES or CRYSTAL KANJIS for particular states
Sense	Zmysł	Sens	must be specified
Song	Pieśń	Chanson	as musical sequence
Trinity	Trójca; Troistość;	Trinité	must be specified
Mind	Umysł	Esprit	Fraction of the Triad: MIND-BODY-SPIRIT
Brain	Mózg	**Cerveau**	as Drawing
Realm	Dziedzina, Królestwo	Domaine; Royaume	as Animation
Chorus; Choir	Chór	Chœur	**χορός(CHORUS)** **GREEK**
Sign	**Znak**	Signe	↻CRYS TAL BASIC

\

			ECHO
UNIVERSAL			Universal
UNIVERSAL			**Κόσμος (KOSMOS)** **GREEK**
Soul	**Dusza**	Âme	usually in the Triad: MIND-BODY-SPIRIT
UNIVERSAL			**KARMA (KARMAN)** - from Sanskritकर्म
UNIVERSAL			**Βυθός(BYT HOS)**
Infinity	Nieskończoność	Infini	∞ - Maths
World	**Świat**	Monde	must be specified
Vision	**Wizja**	Vision	must be specified
Vibe	Wibracja	Ambiance	
Horizon	Horyzont	Horizon	as <Borderline>in CRYSTAL BASIC

Reality	**Rzeczywist ość**	Réalité	must be defined in CRYSTAL BASIC
Dream	Sen, Marzenie	**Songe**	CRY STAL BASIC
Boundary	Granica	Frontière	**LIMES-** Maths
Earth	**Ziemia**	Terre	☿ - Universal
quote French		**Élan** = <*Élan vital*>	*pulsation*
Moon	Księżyc	**Lune**	☽ - Universal
Star	Gwiazda	**Étoile**	* - Universal
Poet	Poeta	Poète	as Λ with radiation
Unknown	Niewiadom a	**Inconnue**	x - Maths
Machine	Maszyna	Machine	must be specified

\

Universe	**Wrzechświat**	Univers	variation of **Κόσμος (KOSMOS)**
Space	**Przestrzeń**	Espace	Part of (Time-Space) Check also Chinese – 宇宙 *yuzhou*
Time	Czas	Temps	as above
	Universal		**Big Bang -** Physics
Model	**Model**	Modèle	in <3 D >
Art	Sztuka	Art	**ARS -** Latin
Tree	**Drzewo**	Arbre	drawing
Animal	**Zwierzę**	Animal	must be specified
Night	Noc	**Nuit**	- Crystal Basic
Light	Światło	Lumière	**LUX**- Latin

Predator	Drapieżnik	Prédateur	must be specified
Fear,	Strach,	Peur	**FOBIA** - Universal
Death	Śmierć	**Mort**	Fraction of of
	UNIVERSAL		**SEX**
Hunter	Łowca	Chasseur	must be specified
Lotus	Lotos	Lotus	drawing
Wisdom	Mądrość	Sagesse	as <Crystal Insight>
Memory	Pamięć	Mémoire	as specific Crystals
Unconscio usness	Nieświado mość	Inconscienc e	Fraction of <Triple Awareness: Unconscious - Subconscious>
Subconscio usness	Podświado mość	Sous- Conscience	as above
Cell	Komórka	Cellule	drawing
	UNIVERSAL		**YIN**

UNIVERSAL			YANG
Strength	**Siła**	Force	
Verbs (mostly conjugated as in the Reading)			
speak	mówi	**parle**	
fills	wypełnia	**remplie**	
breathes	oddycha	**respire**	
learns, knows	zna, poznaje	**connaît**	
presents, discovers	**objawia**	présente, découvre	
fights, struggles	**walczy**	lutte, se bat,	
inspires	**inspiruje**	inspire	
drives	kieruje, prowadzi	conduit, impulse	
perceives	postrzega	**perçoit**	
produces	tworzy, rodzi	**produit**	
defines	definiuje	**definit**	

appears	pojawia się	**apparaît**	
ejaculates	**wytryska**	éjacule	
exists	istnieje	**existe**	
sails	żegluje	**navire**	
presents	przedstawia	**représente**	
operates	działa	fonctionne	
builds	buduje	**construit**	
revolves	okrąża	gravite	
fulfills	spełnia się	s'accomplie	
evolves	ewoluuje	évolue	
breathes	oddycha	respire	
blinks	migocze	clignote	
understands	**pojmuje**	comprends	
travels	**podróżuje**	voyage	
dream	śni	**rêve**	

flies	leci	**vol**	
escapes	ucieka	s'échappe	
sees	**widzi**	voit	
begins	zaczyna się	**commence**	
sings	śpiewa	**chante**	
dances	tańczy	danse	
responds	odpowiada	**réponds**	
jumps	skacze	sauts	**333**
vibrates	**wibruje**	vibre	
unifies	jednoczy się	**s'unifie**	
composes	**komponuje**	compose	
bears	**poczyna**	procrée	
enters	wkracza	**entre**	
lasts	trwa	dure	
discovers	**odkrywa**	révèle	

projects	wyświetla	projets	
finds	znajduje	**trouve**	

Other Parts of Speech

superconsci ous	**nadświado my**	superconsci ent	
	Universal		META
	Universal		NEO*
unknown	**nieznany**	Inconnu	
conscious	świadomy	conscient	
far	daleko	**loin**	
inside	**wewnątrz**	dedans	
harmonious ly	**harmonijni e**	harmonieus ement	
now	**teraz**	maintenant	
here	tutaj	**ici**	
outside	na zewnątrz	**dehors**	
inspired	**natchniony**	inspiré	

fabulous	**baśniowo**	fabuleux	
fantasticall y	fantastyczni e	fantastique ment	
creatively	kreatywnie	**créativeme nt**	
still; yet	jeszcze	**encore**	
rhythmically	**rytmicznie**	rythmiquem ent	
beyond	poza	au-delà	
bounlessly	**bezgranicz nie**	infiniment	
always	zawsze	toujours	
eternally	**wiecznie**	éternelleme nt	
everywhere	**wszędzie**	partout	
cyclically	cyklicznie	cycliqueme nt	
biologically	**biologiczni e**	biologiquem ent	
irrationally	**irracjonalni e**	irrationelle ment	
magically	**magicznie**	magiqueme nt	
visually	wizualnie	visuellemen t	

misteriously	tajemniczo	mistérieusement	
slowly	powoli	lentement	
strangely	**dziwnie**	étrangement	
nothing	**nic**	rien	
rarely	**rzadko**	rarement	
electrically	**elektrycznie**	électriquement	
new	**nowy**	nouveau	
organically	**organicznie**	organiquement	
Past; past	Przeszłość; przeszły	**Passé; passé**	
Future; future	Przyszłość; przyszły	**Futur; future**	
Crystal; crystal	Kryształ; kryształowy	**Cristal; cristallin**	
Center; in the middle	Centrum; w środku	**Centre; centre**	

\

Books of SUDOKU SET

by **MJS, Mac 333 & Master InOut**

The Trilogy

BOOK 2

BOOK OF DUALITY - Road Down The Hill

BOOK 4

BOOK OF 4 TIME-SPACES - *w w w w*

BOOK 8

BOOK OF ANALEMMA - *Eight Minutes*

The Triptych

BOOK 6

CLOCKWISE ROTATIONS - *Rune 6*

BOOK 3

BOOK OF TRINITY - *Third Eclipse*

BOOK 9

COUNTERCLOCKWISE ROTATIONS - *Rune 9*

The Ternion

BOOK 7

BOOK OF FRACTAL TIME - *Seven TS Crystals*

BOOK 5

BOOK OF PENTAGAME - *Fifth Axis*

BOOK 1

BOOK OF SINGULARITY - *Bardo*

\

www.ingramcontent.com/pod-product-compliance
Lightning Source LLC
Chambersburg PA
CBHW070945050326
40689CB00014B/3349